THE
SEARCH
FOR LOST
FATHERING

The
SEARCH
FOR LOST
FATHERING

● ●

Rebuilding Your Father Relationship

JAMES L. SCHALLER

Fleming H. Revell
A Division of Baker Book House
Grand Rapids, Michigan 49516

Published by Fleming H. Revell
a division of Baker Book House Company
P.O. Box 6287, Grand Rapids, MI 49516-6287

Printed in the United States of America

Library of Congress Cataloging-in-Publication Data

Schaller, James L.
    The search for lost fathering : rebuilding your father relationship / James L. Schaller.
      p. cm.
    Includes bibliographical references.
    ISBN 0-8007-5552-9
    1. Father and child. 2. Fatherhood—Religious aspects—Christianity. I. Title.
HQ755.85.S34 1995
306.874′2—dc20   94-37752

To my best man and father
James A. Schaller, M.D.

In appreciation for
nice memories of eating at Kelly's,
long hours delivering babies at Nazareth Hospital,
which paid for those memories,
not running from our problems,
trying to learn new tricks,
talking me out of medicine—
did you really expect me to listen?
being one heck of a good potato pancake maker—
was your heart attack planned?
and for the privilege of
life

Contents

· · · · · · · · · · · · · · ·

Acknowledgments

• •

*L*et me list those worthy of special thanks.

My sister, Maureen Schaller Ruth, for sacrificial, late night editing, understanding all that I write, and being a "soul sister."

The library staff at the Eastern Pennsylvania Psychiatric Institute: Kathleen Turner, Randall S. Blackwell, Kathy Davis, and Lenore Hardy. Your amazing computer wizardry, professionalism in research, and constant helpfulness have been priceless. And the affection and joking has made your library a friendly oasis in the middle of the day.

The library staff at Westminster Theological Seminary, especially Phil Monroe, who was able to draw upon his psychology and theology training and see the goal. He was a tireless research assistant and taught me a great deal. My appreciation also to Jane Patete for her many kindnesses over the years. Thank you for calculating due dates in years instead of weeks.

The Fleming H. Revell editors were very supportive. William Petersen, Mary Suggs, Dave Wimbish, Bob Hostetler, and Sharon Van Houten— thanks for the sweat, patience, and polish. And, Bill, thanks for believing.

Professor Patrick Keane of LeMoyne College and Wes and Vicki Flemming who repeatedly corrected my writing over the years, and to Professors Harvie Conn, Sinclair Ferguson, and Clair Davis of Westminster, for ideas worth writing down.

My appreciation to my old friends at Teen Challenge in Syracuse, particularly Dave Pilch and Mike Delaney.

David McCray of West Virginia for typing the earliest chapters and Dr. Ed Welsh, Dr. Doug Schoeninger, Charles Zeidos, Marisa Morelli,

Marianne Schaller, Dr. Michele Novotni, Bob Novotni, Dick and Anne Swartley, and Steve Blake for reading them.

Friends from Church of the Savior and Life Counseling Services, particularly Gene Girard, Dr. Tom Whiteman, the Malones, Gary Donahue, Nancy Cellucci, and Dan "the Russian Ambassador" Knezevich.

Dr. Ralph Eckardt for years of support "in the worst of times."

Joyce, my dearest sweetheart and wife, for much editorial wisdom, and more importantly, for a level of friendship and intimacy I never dreamed was possible.

Part 1

The Importance of the Father-Child Relationship

1

Everybody Needs a Father

. . . .

*J*essica was not the girl I had imagined she would be. Having heard some frightening details of her story from my nurse, I had assumed she would be hostile and reactive—a test of my patience. But as she walked quietly into my office and took a seat, I saw that she was a sweet eleven-year-old, the type of daughter who would make any parent proud.

She greeted me respectfully and asked to be called "Red" (which struck me as curious, since her hair appeared more brown than red). She faithfully followed all my directions during our chat, and never once complained. The child obviously had a dash of shyness, but she was able to talk about her feelings—our staff therapist had been a benefit. When I told her that our team was pleased with her progress, she smiled warmly.

I found it hard to believe that just three weeks earlier, this same girl had taken a knife and chased her mother around the house, saying, "I'm going to kill you!"

At that time, she had been living with her mother. Her parents had separated because of her father's alcohol problem; nevertheless, they had come to an agreement that Jessica's father, who was also nicknamed "Red," could see her three times a month, as long as he didn't drink during the visits. Red followed this agreement faithfully for five months, during which time father and daughter regularly talked on the phone, bowled, played games, and even went to Red's softball games.

But then he broke the agreement.

One weekend while Jessica was at her father's apartment, a group of guys came by to watch a football game on TV. They brought beer, and the temptation was too much for Red. When Jessica's mom called to adjust the time she would pick up her daughter, she could tell that Red was mildly intoxicated. Moments later, while Jessica was reveling in the attention of five loud, exuberant men, her mother burst into the apartment and angrily pulled her off the couch and rushed her out to the car.

When they got home, Jessica was told to go wash the dishes piled up in the sink. Her mother had planned to discuss the event over dinner, but Jessica was seething over what her mother had done to her. Somewhere deep in her heart, she felt her basic need for a father's love being thwarted, even assaulted. She could not face losing her father, so she attacked her mother, threatening to kill her with a knife.

Certainly, Jessica's story is extreme. But she is not alone in her hunger for fathering. Jessica's act was wrong, but it is profoundly telling. It points to a need in all of us. Each of us longs for a father's love and acceptance.

Life distracts us. We forget or are unaware of the basic experiences of our past that have shaped and now control us. Sometimes we do not perceive the problem in our father relationship. We need our fathers to be special and good, so we stuff our bad father experiences deep down inside. Father failures hurt too much to face. The mistakes fathers make may be subtle and hard to pinpoint, but they still have immense impact on the lives of their children.

So where do we start? Perhaps with the questions that are behind the title of this book: Do you feel a loss in your father relationship? Does something feel wrong with it? Do you hunger for something that your father relationship should satisfy but doesn't?

Emotional Signs of Father Hunger

Many people have a void inside them that is due to "father hunger," and this disguised hunger has had great impact on the way they live. Do any of these statements apply to you?

- When I think about my father I become emotional—insecure, sad, or angry.

- When I'm with my father I don't act like myself; I'm either childish or grandiose.
- I consider my father wonderful, but others think I'm fooling myself.
- I feel numb toward my father.
- I have trouble with competitiveness.
- My motivation is poor because I feel beaten down.
- I have difficulty establishing relationships.
- I move too quickly into new relationships.
- I'm confused about my identity—it's not as if my father ever made me feel good about myself.
- I don't feel like a real man.
- I lack confidence in my femininity.
- I feel unattractive.
- I feel incompetent.
- It is difficult for me to relax.
- I have problems with my sexuality.
- Being assertive is hard for me.
- People seem to feel that I violate their boundaries.
- I'm afraid to get too close to others.
- I fear being abandoned.
- Authority makes me uneasy.
- My father's criticism hurt me too much. Now I have difficulty accepting criticism.
- God often feels a million miles away.
- I have little interest in spirituality.
- When my father does not provide the emotional support my mother needs, my mother unknowingly tries to get me to provide that support.
- My father confides in me too much.
- My father and I do not talk openly and honestly about our lives.
- I keep trying to please everybody—especially father-types or mentors.
- I run to things and people to nurse myself in a compulsive way.
- I am rarely satisfied.
- I live with a vague, diffused fearfulness.

- I am a parent who worries I am repeating my father's and grand-father's mistakes.
- Sometimes I feel like an orphan.

The conditions listed above are often associated with incomplete father relationships. The absence of a mature father-child connection creates a void in the soul, a residual "father hunger."

Father hunger is the result of receiving too little quality fathering as a child or young adult. Some argue that even grown men and women need fathers or father surrogates and that the absence of such role modeling and support is associated with less fulfillment in life. Father hunger also results from too little intimacy between child and father.

Over the last ten years, I have witnessed during counseling sessions the depth of the hunger men and women feel for fathering. Even those in their sixties and seventies have told me of the hunger and longing they still feel. And often the need is hidden, like a deep river of water flowing under the surface. The hunger may be out of sight but it is never gone. I know this from having heard hundreds of people tell me what they want from life. After we get beyond the superficial they say something like, "I want my father to call and talk to me" or "I want my father to stop drinking and come home. I need him so much."

After more time, the deepest waters break through to the surface. The hunger, longing, and disappointments begin to come forth. "I wish my dad were alive." "Dad, I feel so weak without you." "I wish my dad weren't sick so I could lean on him the way I used to." And so it goes.

Most of these people are highly functioning members of their communities. They are respected in their relationships. They are responsible employees. Nevertheless, they obviously have unresolved pain associated with their fathers. They thirst for "father water."[1] They have been left with a void, an injury, a psychic thirst that only a father can quench. I am becoming increasingly convinced that this is nearly universal.

In this book you may be surprised to see the extent of your father's role in your most cherished relationships, your vocation, your satisfaction with life, and your experience of God. I will try to walk with you through what may be intense topics, but in the end I hope you will feel less controlled by the past and have direction for further healing.

Father Deficiency

For the purposes of this book, I have identified two levels of father deficiency: obvious deficiency and broad deficiency. Obvious father deficiency has various causes. A father may die before his children reach adulthood. Some fathers desert their children and leave their families to function alone—often in poverty. Divorce causes 40 percent of all children to spend at least part of their growing-up years in a single parent family, and most of these children will have minimal contact with their fathers.[2]

Sophia Loren is a vivid example of obvious father deficiency. Her life illustrates how fathers impact our love life and marriage choice.

Sophia saw her father only a few times. He put in an appearance at the hospital when she was born, acknowledged that he was her father, and immediately departed. Having seduced Sophia's mother, he now abandoned both mother and child, leaving them to face the shame and humiliation heaped upon them by others in their small Italian town.

When Sophia was five years old she met her father for the first time. Her mother, upon hearing the news that he was coming to see Sophia, became nervous and excited, fussing over the child's hair and dress so she would be as attractive as possible. Sophia remembers that he was tall and handsome, and that he gave her a toy car—a beautiful blue race car with her name painted on the side. After she received it, she ran up to her room in tears. Despite all the lavish gifts she has received, Sophia Loren says that little blue car still holds a special place in her memory.[3]

In her teen years, Sophia tried to fill in the hole left by her absent father. "I was busy working on films. . . . I was the head of the family, going out to work everyday, my mother was the wife, and my sister, now back in school, was the child."[4]

As an adult, though, Sophia still longed for her father, despite the pain he had caused her. On one occasion her sister had arranged a visit at their father's home. He was ill and weak and her sister, Maria, wanted Sophia to see him before it was too late. He took her through his flat, and even showed her his favorite mementos. When she was getting ready to leave, he took one of her hands and said, "I am very proud of you."[5]

Yet even this good memory brings heartache. Because her father's "I am very proud of you" was the only affectionate thing he ever said to her, it stands alone in a sea of silence.

"Growing up in a small Neapolitan town," she reveals, "it was the dream of my life to have a father." Trying to get over the immense sense of rejection from having been left, she tried to find him in other men. She spent her life seeking surrogates for him—in Carlo Ponti, the husband who fathers her, and in older actors and directors who remind her in some way of the father she never "won."[6]

Sophia is quite frank and pleasantly transparent about her choice of a husband. In her late teens she was aware of a deep need to be loved. She had met Ponti when she was fifteen, and by the time she was nineteen they were seriously involved. He was forty-one and married, but he soon divorced his wife so he could marry Sophia.

She said, "I suppose he's the father I never had, the father I needed in my life. Even now. I'm forty-four, but the little, shy, illegitimate, fatherless girl of Pozzuoli is still very much inside of me, and I need the father of Carlo as much today as I ever did."[7]

In her autobiography, one sees signs of her understanding and healing. Sophia had the courage to examine herself, and the benefit is obvious. She can look at her life and admit to herself: "I sought him everywhere. I married him. I made my best films with him. I curried his favor. I sat on his lap and snuggled him. . . . I saw him only a few times . . . yet he dominated my life."[8] She wrote her life story to come to terms with him, to separate the delusions from the truth. And it seems, by extension, to find a stable identity. At least in her life there was a clear starting point. She knew she had a father deficiency because he clearly was gone. What about homes with a father who is emotionally gone? To express the pain of children in these families we need another broader definition of father deficiency.

Broad deficiency occurs when a father lives at home but provides little or no quality parenting. For example, fathers who abuse alcohol or drugs may be unable to have positive relationships with their children. Their behavior may be disruptive to the family, causing financial problems, and forcing the children into overwhelming levels of responsibility early in life.[9]

In this way an alcoholic father can undermine the emotional health of all family members. Such fathers are "anti-fathers," psychic black holes who consume the strength and childhoods of their children. This is also true of sexually and physically abusive fathers.

For example, it has been estimated that as many as 5 percent of all girls are sexually abused by their fathers.[10] One researcher believes that sexual abuse victimizes a million children each year, with physical abuse claiming a similar number. More recent figures show the real numbers are probably even higher. Much of this abuse is inflicted by fathers. Many fathers who would not physically abuse their children nonetheless abuse them verbally, through ridicule and insults.

Some adult children are controlled by insecure fathers and feel unable to choose their own path through life. Some cannot connect with Dad because his standards are considered severe and impossible to obtain— he expects too much beauty, morality, academic or athletic prowess, or artistic ability. Some are denied active fathering because their fathers are weak and ill with chronic illnesses like Alzheimer's disease, stroke, cancer, diabetes, and heart or lung disease. Many adult children, especially daughters, are stepping in and caring for the man they once looked to as a defender and provider. Such a role reversal, even if appropriate, is much like a funeral. For example, a demented father can never help his child again. In fact, he has become her child—at this point she is clearly on her own and functionally fatherless.

Probably the most common source of father deficiency involves fathers who isolated themselves from intimacy with their children by excess work during the children's formative first two decades. Even as retired men these fathers may continue to be emotionally absent from their families ,leaving many of their children with an emotional void.

Men have been taught in American culture that real men don't cry or show affection. Subsequently, we have generations of children who have almost never received affection or experienced emotional closeness with their fathers.

Years of counseling have shown me that often those who say they have great father relationships are the most troubled. It is common to use idealization to hide the reality of an unpleasant relationship. Sometimes in my work I have discovered that the child who is close to Dad may actually have been very hurt by his or her father's intensity in the relationship. The difference between overwhelming intensity and appropriate involvement is very subtle. An example of this can be seen by examining the life's work of composer Charles Ives. His father was a good parent by many standards, yet he controlled the entire life course of his talented child, even from the grave. Ives's story indicates that even a genius may live a life largely governed by a troubled connection to his father.

Charles Ives has been called "the most original and inventive, and possibly the greatest" composer in American history.[11] He was born in 1874 in Connecticut, the son of George Ives, an energetic bandleader. George was an intense lover of music, and spent hours trying to pass on his passion to his son, making sure that the boy learned how to play a number of instruments. Charles identified profoundly with his father, taking up George's wildly experimental, inventive style of composing.[12]

Most people, on hearing of a father and son spending so much time together, smile in approval. But there is more to the story. Indeed, some people wonder if Charles was not overwhelmed by his father, perhaps even abused by the man's emotional intensity.

During Charles's college years, a number of conflicts developed between him and his father. Unfortunately, George died at the age of forty-nine before these conflicts could be resolved. Charles's feelings of anger and sadness were poorly worked through, and it appears he coped with his father loss by decades of idealization.

After his father's death, the music of his father filled his mind, perhaps haunting him, and he began to write constantly—utilizing every bit of his spare time to create music.

As Stuart Feder compellingly demonstrates in his book, *My Father's Song*, Ives's music was an "unconscious creative collaboration" with his deceased father, a way to mourn without mourning. Charles's songs were filled with references to his father, his father's hymns and marches, his father's eccentric sounds, and the sights that had surrounded them as they played together when Charles was a boy.

After almost thirty years of productive composition, Ives's output began to taper off. Why?

Feder believes that Charles's unconscious identification with his father affected not only the content of Charles's music, but the exact time it ceased. After memorializing his father in his musical compositions, Charles "died," in a sense, in that he allowed his creativity to die. Specifically, when Charles reached the age of forty-eight, he began to pull his works together, publishing them in 1922. The following year, when he was forty-nine (the age at which his father died), Ives's creative impulse died. The length of his father's physical life thus marked the length of Charles's creative life. While many of his materials continued to be performed and praised after this time, nevertheless, in his remaining decades Charles Ives functioned largely as a "cantankerous recluse."[13]

The life of Charles Ives shows that it is often difficult for a child to understand the depths of his father's influence. Ives was a brilliant man but he lacked insight into the effect of his father on him. Though he and his father spent time together, it was not a healthy interaction.

You may think your father was a "good" father, but for your own well-being, you must evaluate the relationship you had and have with him. Some of my patients call their fathers "good" as a way to defend against their "bad" experiences with them. I've heard many abused children quote their fathers as though they are sages. They believe their fathers are "good" because that's better than accepting the dark reality.

Even an involved father may not be a "good" father. Some men have trouble changing from being a protective father of a little child to a mentoring father of a young adult. Many protective fathers struggle to allow a young adult child to develop his own uniqueness, vocation, or parenting style. It's interesting to note that Charles Ives had his conflicts with his father when they stopped playing music together and Charles moved away, showing signs of independence.

Finally, calling a father "good" may be equivalent to saying he was satisfactory, i.e., he was not abusive, paid the bills, and came to birthday parties. Satisfactory may be the norm for American society, but is it good? According to two authors, what is normal is distant fathers who leave their children with feelings of incompleteness.

Victoria Secunda's *Women and Their Fathers* opens with five middle-aged women sharing lunch as they complain about their mothers. After a period of time, Secunda suggests that they chat about their dads. The conversation comes to an abrupt halt. Slowly it dawns on these women that their fathers are largely strangers to them. Sure, these women are able to talk about sterile facts such as their fathers' ages, birthplaces, employment, and health. But on the whole, their fathers seemed amorphous, mythical, and absent. Indeed, just mentioning them induced a "curious amnesia" in their daughters.[14]

Lee Salk's *My Father, My Son* discusses twenty-eight father-son relationships. What is striking about these relationships is the almost universal sense, even among those with kind fathers, that they have not received enough of their fathers' love. All of them felt they needed more.

Secunda and Salk show us that something is missing in father relationships, even in "normal households."

The implications of this father void are not trivial. When I talk to psychologists, social workers, psychiatrists, pastors, priests, pastoral workers, and schoolteachers, I repeatedly hear an emphasis on the need for healing the effects of father deprivation. In subsequent chapters I'll use cases to show the specific effects of such deprivation on your work, love life, emotional struggles, and identity. But you may also be surprised to learn how seriously spirituality can be distorted, blocked, or rendered empty—even among those who are considered spiritual giants, due to trouble with their fathers.

2

The Prize

• • • • • • • • • • • • • • •

I believe with all my heart that for many people the father-child relationship defines their entire lives. It affects their dating and marriage relationships, degree of drivenness, identity, sexuality, and work performance. My goal is to bring insight into the effects of this relationship, and to show the path to health, change, and greater fulfillment.

But there is something else I want to offer, more than insight and healing with your physical father. I want to connect you to the Creator of the universe . . . the Father of your soul.

I'll understand if you want to put the book aside now, to look after other matters. Indeed, I find myself spending all my hours attending to other "weightier" matters, soothing myself with anything other than God. The "plan B" options are endless. Perhaps this is a glimpse at our insanity. We crave what fills for an hour or a day and avoid the mysterious living water from God. Later, we will examine some reasons for our spiritual avoidance and for the walls so many of us erect to keep God out. Perhaps we doubt that God cares for us. Actually, God is reaching out to us, as the case of Marianne dramatically illustrates.

Marianne was a twenty-two-year-old bank teller who considered herself minimally religious. During our difficult counseling work together, it became clear that her hostility and suspicion of me were really directed toward her biological father, whom she had seen only a few times.

One night Marianne had a dream. In it, a man walked toward her and asked, "Who is your father?"

As the question was asked, Marianne saw a round portrait of her biological father hanging on a white wall. Since she had seen the man for only two hours her entire life, she felt uncomfortable identifying him as her father. Yet she saw no other options. So reluctantly and halfheartedly she lifted her hand and pointed to the portrait on the wall.

"I guess that's my father," she said.

"No, Marianne," the man said. "That is not your father."

Marianne was bewildered.

"If that's not my father," she asked, "then who is?"

The man looked lovingly into Marianne's face and said, "I am your father, Marianne. I am the living God."

I suppose some might regard this unusual dream as merely a release of brain energy or conflicting psychological themes. Why such a narrow interpretation? As we shall see later, it is very much in God's character to seek those with orphan feelings. Marianne was a physical and emotional orphan who was so reactive that no one could get close to her—she certainly did not trust me. But God reached out and cared for her, drawing her from her lonely emptiness toward hope.

Marianne's dream is striking. It is a profound thing to witness the birth of a spiritual life—like dawn flashing on the horizon. For even as she first told me about her amazing dream, she was no longer reactive and melancholy, but calm and happy. She still had many problems, but she was never quite the same. She had been pursued in love and had been found. She believed that she would never be alone again, and she laughed with new contentment.

You may not be hurting the way Marianne was hurting. But as you will see, one can have orphan feelings while a parent is still alive. There is healing out there for you too, as much healing as you need to find wholeness and contentment. So I invite you to join me on a journey I began many years ago. The quality of the rest of your life may hang in the balance.

When the Spiritual "Truly" See

Most of us don't have the dramatic dreams that Marianne experienced. Many spiritual people feel they can know God without such experiences, and that is often true. But sometimes people think they believe in God's love and presence only to discover at some point that childhood experiences hinder them from knowing emotionally what they believe intellectually. A powerful confession of Charles Stanley demonstrates this.

At the Second International Christian Counselors Conference, Charles humbly shared that despite his success and popularity as a Christian minister, his spiritual contentment and happiness were hindered for decades by father issues.

Charles's father died when he was seven months old. His mother had to work hard as a single parent, and consequently was often away from home. Charles felt deeply rejected by his parents' absence. His father "walked out" when he died, and his mother was home only at night. Coming home from school he would dread placing his key into the door lock, because he knew there was only profound loneliness on the other side. When other kids talked about their fathers, he felt a vague emotional ache.

His mother sensed his longing for a father, so to provide him with one, she married again when Charles was nine years old. Unfortunately, the boy's new father was bitter and angry over unresolved issues with his own father, and only sprayed hostility and hatred throughout the house. Charles's mother spent her energy dealing with her volatile husband, leaving Charles more lonely than before.

Often his stepfather's frustration and rage were taken out on Charles, who was too young and small to fight back—at first. Because his stepfather was violent toward him and his mother, Charles felt a growing hostility and distrust of authority. Finally, on one occasion his stepfather hit him in the face for some annoying comment, and Charles hit the man back fiercely. Although his stepfather beat him for what he had done, Charles had seen a moment of fear in the man's eyes, and from that moment on he became outright rebellious. In later years, his rebellions even affected his work and ministry.

Charles also developed a bad image of God. His academic theology was good, but his root feelings about God were twisted. God the Father seemed distant, harsh, and unable to be pleased—much like his stepfather.

Because of his dulled experience of God and the emasculating harshness of his father, Charles was left to fight for approval and acceptance. He had no tender father memories to encourage and soothe him, so he fought to make it alone. The solution to every problem was to work harder. He fought to prove his worth to himself and others. He preached more and longer. He tried to pray the most. Charles eagerly sought to show everyone he belonged, that he could do it. His perfectionist standards seeped into his sermon preparations so that even these became a chore. Each new sermon had to be better than the last. If he gave a good sermon one Sunday, it had to be great the next week. Finally, he reached the end of himself.

Exhaustion nearly killed Charles Stanley, and his recovery took a full year, during which time he began to see himself in a new way. He saw how he had tried to force things to work, and he recognized his attempts to win God's acceptance by meeting a perfectionist religious standard—a standard that was always beyond his reach. He saw his excess need to control and win. He saw how critical he had been of others, often assuming that his opinion was correct just because he had prayed over an issue.

By the time Charles Stanley reached his forties he had achieved tremendous success, yet he was discontented—terribly so. He fasted, read books, and attended religious seminars, but nothing helped. His standard answer had been, "God will straighten out any problem—all you've got to do is get on your knees and get in the Word," but he had begun to recognize that simplistic approach as "juvenile." When he did begin to open up and share his emotional struggles he got scared—as if looking inside would cause him to sink into unlimited grief and darkness.

Finally, in desperation, he arranged a meeting with four friends to seek their help. They went on an Oregon mountain retreat to discover what was wrong with Charles. Once there, he shared his life story. He spoke for hours over the course of two days. He began with his earliest memory (of sitting up in bed as a child, crying) and continued to talk of his life up to that day.

When he had finished, his friends spoke for the first time. They made several observations about his story. Finally one man asked Charles to put his head on the table and close his eyes, which he did. His friend then said, "Your father just picked you up in his arms and held you. What do you feel?" Charles burst out crying, and continued to cry for thirty minutes. The sense of his father picking him up felt wonderfully warm. He felt secure and loved. And he cried some more.

Charles began to realize what was wrong. He had always been slightly aware of a wall between God and him. But as he sat with his head down, crying, it occurred to him that he had never *felt* God loving him. He would tell other people that God loved them, and he knew intellectually that God loved him, but he had never felt it. He left the mountains with a new sense of closeness to God. The old wall had finally dissolved.

When he returned to work he pulled out his sermon file on "the love of God." There was only one sermon on God's love in all those years of preaching. He remembered that it was so pitiful that he had only preached it once, whereas most other sermons had been "recycled" several times. It had been bad, he realized, because he hadn't really known what he was talking about. He was a successful minister who could translate the Greek text, but he could not translate God's love into meaningful words. He was a blind man trying to speak about color. Charles had been unable to believe deep down in his heart that God could love him unconditionally. Over time he has come to know he is loved just as he is, that he doesn't need to try to do anything to earn God's fatherly love. That realization changed Charles Stanley's life and work. His experience is typical of those who sincerely search for their lost fathering.

Join me as we start that search.

3

The Search for Lost Fathering

*A*ngela was eight, with stringy brown hair and a wiry frame. She had just started ballet, and was obviously proud of her new white costume.

She was aware that her daddy and his guests were laughing out on the porch, so she thought it would be a great opportunity to show off the routine she had just learned.

Smiling excitedly, she tiptoed onto the porch and into our midst.

Her father glared down at her.

"What are you doing out here?" he demanded.

"I don't know," the little girl whispered, taking a step backwards.

"Didn't I tell you never to interrupt adult conversations?"

"Uh . . . yeah. . . ."

"Now that we have all seen your costume, you can go back inside," he said firmly.

Sadly, with obvious embarrassment, the little girl turned and went back inside the house. We didn't see her again for the rest of the evening.

My heart fell when I saw how Angela's father responded to his little girl's longing for attention. That child needed to know she was important before the world had a chance to knock her down and make her feel like a loser. But instead of giving her the affirmation she needed, her father shamed her in front of his friends. He berated her need to be noticed.

I have met many Angelas in my practice, at my church, and among my friends. They may be adults now, but inside they are still children looking for a father to say, "What a lovely outfit! Could you please show us a few dance steps?" How many adults still ache to hear their father figures and mentors say, "Hey, gang, have you met my wonderful daughter? Boy, do I love her! She's the best!"

Angela went to her room that evening with a bruised heart, emotionally beaten down. Her hunger for affirmation not only remained; it had grown. Being shamed on the porch had only increased her need for encouragement.

As time goes on, things will change for that child. Her body will become a woman's body, her mind that of a woman. Her sense of the profound subtleties of human relationships will grow. She will put herself in positions and relationships that will let her be seen and built up. And, quite possibly, she will spend the rest of her life trying to earn the kind words she missed that day on the porch.

John is driven by the same desire. In a group setting he usually tries to answer every question, even if he really doesn't know the answer. He draws the attention of the group to himself because he needs others to praise him. Why? As I have gotten to know John and hear him talk about his father, I have learned that in John's experience for every kind word that came from his father's lips, there were at least three critical ones. John has been seeking approval since he was a little boy, trying to heal himself and show that his father's devaluing comments were wrong. John's actions say to the group, "Please notice me and tell me I'm special." Yet John is no longer a child; he is forty-eight years old.

Someone may protest that I am making too much of the father-child relationship. After all, a father is only one person among many who shape a child's identity. While that's true, it's also true that for many children their father has nearly defined their identity. And we are wrong if we think years or success cause us to outgrow our desire for a father's encouragement.

For example, I remember a restaurant owner, Tommy, who told me about the day he bought a brand-new Lexus. He went out to dinner with his parents and girlfriend, and after dinner, he went out to the parking lot to get the car. He began walking faster and faster to get to his car, finally breaking into a trot.

"Why am I running like this?" he asked himself. He felt ashamed of his behavior. *I'm thirty-eight years old,* he thought. *Why am I acting this way?*

As he and I discussed the incident, the answer emerged. Tommy's parents had parked on the opposite end of the street, and he wasn't sure they would wait with his girlfriend while he brought the car around. He was running because he wanted to make sure his father saw his fancy new car. Surely, he reasoned, if his father saw the sort of car he was driving, the man would admire and respect him.

But that's not what happened. His father's reaction was negative: "Never thought I'd see you in something like that. Bet the payments are a nightmare, huh? Well, hope you enjoy it anyway."

Tommy was deflated by his father's reaction, of course. But then again, his father had always been much freer with the insults than the praise—and so, even as a thirty-eight-year-old man, Tommy was still looking to his father for what he had never received as a child, and he was still coming up empty.

Why do fathers matter so much to people like Tommy? Why can't they be satisfied with a blessing from their mothers? The answer may have to do with a father's role in developing his children's identities.

Fathers and Uncertain Identities

A child begins life united to his (or her) mother. The child literally is fused into his mother's body. Even after birth, the infant is singularly dependent on his mother; she is the source of his nourishment and security. Over time, however, the child learns that the mother is a separate person—a potentially frightening realization, because independence means that you can be alone.

So where does the father enter in? In past decades, he was considered an outsider to the mother-child fusion, and referred to as the first "outsider." In many homes, the job of raising infants and young children was traditionally delegated to the mother; fathers represented "the world," the part of experience that was "out there," beyond the front yard of our homes.

However, in recent years fathers have come to be seen as capable of bonding very early with their infants. In fact, researchers say that whoever cares for the child's physical needs in a tender and appropriate way will be noticed by the child.[1] Burlingham notes that even in the mother-child act of breast-feeding, the child can be looking up at the father while suckling.[2] This means that infants can get messages from their fathers and may bond very early with them—if the men are tender and nurturing. But while it is possible for men to bond with infants, such tender intimacy is rare.

A child's father is typically the first male to write his thoughts and feelings on his child's heart. Fathers, therefore, need to be sensitive to the messages their every word and action inscribe on that tender surface. Their children enter the world like tiny sponges, ready to absorb every little impression about themselves and their identity. They are unsure of who they are: *Am I special?* they ask. *Am I valuable? Am I good? Am I merely an annoyance?* Their fathers play a primary role in answering those questions.

Last month I was playing golf with a close friend when he hit a ball into the water hazard. (I suppressed the urge to dance, and managed a sympathetic look.) Later, he hit another ball into the water.

"Joe," he muttered to himself, "you are as brainless as a crow." On the final hole he hit the ball into the woods and said the same thing.

After the game I asked him where he picked up the "brainless as a crow" expression. He said he wasn't sure; we dropped it, and the conversation turned to other things.

A few days later I was at a party when Joe's older sister dropped a paper plate full of goodies onto the carpet. Her immediate response was to scold herself for being—you guessed it—"brainless as a crow."

Naturally, I asked her about that unusual saying. She paused for a moment, and then remembered that it was something her father had always said to her when she was "bad." Today, these two adults still belittle themselves with the same words their father used, even though the man has been dead for twenty-five years.

This demonstrates the degree to which the words and actions of our fathers affect our identities. Our fathers are carried around inside us long after they have died. We continue to model them, dialogue with them, and listen to them, even after they have been gone for decades. Many of us continue to mirror the image of ourselves that our fathers have written on our souls.

Individuals who did not receive a supportive self-definition from their fathers when they were children can sometimes feel insecure and easily shaken. Those who did receive encouragement and support are more apt to stand strong in the face of life's raging storms.

Jean is a ten-year-old who has a pale face framed by rather unflattering glasses. She is not especially outgoing, but the kids in her school and neighborhood seem to love her.

Jean's father spends a good deal of time at home with his family. He is considerate and respectful to his wife, and he is constantly holding and praising his daughter. He laughs a lot and seems to genuinely enjoy his daughter's company. My impression is that she first faced the world with this message on her internal blackboard: "I am fun. People like to hold and hug me. I have value just as I am."

People who enter the world feeling valued have a benefit that is not often recognized. Others respond differently to them than they do to those with fragile identities. Why? Because individuals project a "spirit," an "identity" that people pick up. For example, the child who enters a new playground thinking, "I am worthless, and nobody will like me," often finds the other kids treating him as if he *is* worthless. And, as Jean illustrates, the reverse can be true. People pick up her contentment and security, and they treat her accordingly.

But many people do not have Jean's sense of wholeness and cohesion, and Cathy is a prime example. I met her after she had attempted suicide.

Unlike many suicidal patients, Cathy did not appear to have any clear signs of a biological depression. She had experienced no weight loss or gain, no fatigue, no problems concentrating, no sleep irregularities, and no appetite changes. After I ruled out biological depression, we talked about her life. It seemed clear to me that her sense of identity was dissolving because her husband had asked her for a divorce. She could not think of being alone; that was "impossible," she said. As we talked further about her marriage, it became evident that her husband had provided her the love and attention her father had never given her.

Cathy's father had worked ten to twelve hours a day as a corporate salesman, and was often on the road for days at a time. When he was home he was emotionally unavailable. She said he was typically grouchy and irritable, "like he would be much happier if we weren't there."

Her mother had also felt alienated by the man, and had looked to her children to be her friends. Cathy found her mother's behavior too stifling and emotionally incestuous, and she wanted out of the house. At the age of twenty-three, Cathy met Tim, a man who seemed to be able to provide the "out" she wanted.

When I asked her about the events just prior to her suicide attempt, she said softly, "Tim asked me to come into the dining room. He said, 'I suppose now is as good a time as any to tell you this. . . .'"

She caught her breath and continued, "When he says this I'm freaking out thinking 'Oh, no, what's this all about?' I got really scared, and I could barely follow him because I was so tense. His face looked so hard. He'd been distant before, but this was different." She stopped to wipe her eyes.

"He told me he wanted a divorce."

After a few minutes, she went on. "I can't live without him. Please help me get him back. I'll never make it by myself!"

Cathy is grieving the loss of a spouse, of course; but she is also experiencing the dissolving of her psychological self. Her identity is like a puzzle board with each piece held in place with glue—and Tim is the glue. Because her father, the first key male in her life, was emotionally absent, she was unable to get glue from him. She entered the dating arena looking for someone to glue her fragile identity together. Tim played that role for a while, but now he is gone, and her identity is fragmenting—like a puzzle knocked off the table and onto the floor.

Pam's situation illustrates the same principle in a more subtle manner. Her father and mother were divorced when she was five, and she sees her dad two or three times a year when he is "in town" on business. In our last session, we talked about her employer, a professor at a local university, whom she has known for three years.

"I'm bummed out today," she told me.

"Why is that?"

"Dr. Reynolds and I aren't getting along all that well. My job's just not as fulfilling as it used to be."

I was under the impression that she had been satisfied with her work, but we hadn't discussed it much. As we talked further about her week, she mentioned that her father had unexpectedly come to town and invited her to lunch. She described their lunch as "annoying."

Then, when she returned to work, she felt that Dr. Reynolds was responding to her differently.

"We went over some class handouts and a research proposal, and I had this sense that he didn't like me—like he wished he had another secretary. He was critical and distracted. I don't know . . . I just didn't want to be there working with him."

A general pattern emerged over the months that followed. Pam became more sensitive after a difficult visit with her father. After time with her dad, if she was criticized, it would hurt more than usual. If affirmation and praise stopped flowing toward her, she became insecure and needy. Her father shook her identity. When her father flew out of town, it seemed he left with Pam's confidence.

Pam was often able to get Dr. Reynolds to help restore it. He was able to glue her back together with his encouragement and attention. She loved it when he was "nice." But she hated it when he was "too business-like." When he criticized her, even for legitimate reasons, she experienced it as a catastrophe, because she needed him to hold her together and make her feel whole.

We all need people to support and affirm us, of course. But Pam's unresolved identity issues were causing her to relate to her employer inappropriately. She longed for his affirmation after her father's visits, and when Dr. Reynolds did not supply it, she lost interest in the job, and in him.

My sense is that many people do what Pam did. They seek to heal their father issues in unproductive ways. They overwhelm a spouse, their friends, mentors, or work associates. Sometimes their hunger to feel valued causes them to join abusive groups and unsound or manipulative religious organizations in an effort to find loyal acceptance and self-worth. They run to substances like alcohol, drugs, and excess food, or try to fill their void with a "high" from compulsive exercise or self-debasing sexual experiences. They work themselves mercilessly because they hope that achievement will earn them a sense of value and self-respect—something their fathers never gave them.

It is not merely a child's identity that a father influences, but also his or her life goals, motivation, sexuality, and relationships with other people.

Go Ahead and Hurt Me—I Deserve It

"Why won't she leave him?"

One of my staff asked me that question once about one of my clients who was in an abusive relationship. One often hears of people who are repeatedly abused, yet decide to stay with the abuser. Why do they endure such treatment? While I believe the answer to that question has many elements, part of the answer relates to identity. Your self-concept dictates, to a great extent, how you allow people to treat you.

Julie illustrates this principle. She was sexually molested by her father from the time she was eight until she was twelve. When she finally became able to talk about it, she asked, "What was it about me that caused him to pick me over my sisters? There were four of us, and he picked me out."

That was the wrong question. It sounds as if her experience has made her embrace a masochistic vision of herself. The real question was, "Why did my father engage in sexual abuse?" But children see the world in terms of themselves. A child's mind reasons, "Bad happens because I did something to cause it—because 'I stepped on a crack,' or 'I was bad.'" Like many children, Julie felt she was being abused because of some personal defect, though the defect, of course, was her father's.

Unfortunately, as Julie entered adulthood she emotionally disconnected herself from the abuse. She treated her father as if nothing had happened, and tried to live as though nothing had happened. But it *had* happened, and it affected the way she let others treat her. For example, she regularly let her roommate violate their rental agreement, and when a conflict arose, Julie readily accepted blame, even when her roommate paid the rent two weeks late or invited guests for a weekend without consulting Julie.

Julie endures such abuse because of the "lessons" she learned from her father. His behavior "taught" her to expect such behavior as a child; consequently, she endures it as an adult. When she was a child she was too young and too small to resist her father, but that is no longer the case. Julie needs to confront her father, and come to terms with the effects of that relationship. Only then will she treat herself with respect—and expect such treatment from others.

Eddie is a college English teacher in his forties. He once heard me speak on father-child relationships and decided to come for counseling.

We talked about his disappointment with his work and about his father's worsening lung cancer.

Eddie wanted a greater closeness with his father before he died. He did not understand why he felt angry towards his father. How can I be angry with a man who is weak with cancer? he asked himself. Eddie also thought of all the fun they had had in recent years watching football together. It didn't make sense.

Eddie started a journal in an attempt to understand his confusing emotions. As he journaled, his mind often turned to his childhood years. He kept seeing mental pictures of his father sitting around the house looking sad and disappointed, a mood that filled the house.

When Eddie was a child, his father would often complain angrily that Eddie had left his room a mess, or that he was doing his chores improperly. Eddie also had the sense that when they ate dinner together, his father was not especially enjoying his company.

He believed that he was somehow responsible for his father's unhappiness and felt that he must have been flawed to cause his father to be so depressed and irritable. As we talked about it, Eddie realized that he had generalized his father's nagging and complaining to mean that his father had rejected him as a person.

"I always sort of thought he loved me," Eddie explained. "Later in life, we became quite free in our words of affection. But I think it has to do with an overall impression."

"What do you mean?" I asked.

"When I was young, he'd get angry at the work I did on the house. The painting was sloppy, the windows weren't clean enough, the dishes weren't washed promptly enough. When I was older, he didn't like any of the girls I dated. Then, when I was married and had two kids of my own, he didn't like the way I was raising them. I don't know. What's the point?" He sighed deeply.

"What's the bottom-line message you take away from this?" I asked.

"That I'm stupid and he wished I hadn't been around."

You see, a double layer of communication was going on between the two men. In recent years they had developed the capacity to express their love for each other, yet other messages had been communicated by decades of disagreement and disapproval. Unpleasant verbal and non-verbal communication from the father in the past carried more weight than more recent positive communication. The message of four decades was far stronger than the recent warmer words between them. These insights helped explain the alienation the son felt. In the months prior to the older man's death, Eddie was able to discuss his unhappy earlier dealings with his father. After some tense conversations, Eddie and his father slowly achieved a greater intimacy and understanding. When Eddie's father finally died, Eddie had closure in their relationship.

Much Like My Father

Ken's relationship with his father is threatened by the elder man's tendency to criticize his son. For example, last year his father came to a party at Ken's house. While Ken was barbecuing the chicken his father made a big deal about the poor job he was doing.

"You're letting the chicken burn!" he said. "Did you marinate it?" "You'd better get those flames out." Ken told me he got so mad at his father he wanted to "punch his lights out."

But for all his indignation toward his father, Ken treats his own family the way his father treats him. During a family therapy meeting, his older children said he is "a chip off the old block." They say he is controlling, opinionated, and critical, not only toward them, but toward his wife as well.

I see this pattern again and again: The children who resent their father's behavior often unknowingly mimic that behavior. It seems to be a natural tendency. When a child is hurt by his father, he relates to others the way his father related to him. But there is an additional psychological principle that may contribute to why Ken could be considered "a chip off the old block."

Leonard Shergold explains the mechanism that can cause someone to identify with an abusive father in his book, *Soul Murder: The Effects of Childhood Abuse and Deprivation.* Overwhelmed by the sheer power of the adult, and utterly dependent, the child is emotionally crushed. The child must have a "good" parent, and therefore, sees the parent's bad acts as "good" or legitimate.[3] In other words, if the only person the child can depend on to protect and defend him is cruel and abusive, the child tries to justify the cruelty. The alternative, that there is really no one to protect and defend him, is just too hard to take.

There is hope for hurting children, though. Abuse does not have to be repeated. Decades of criticism and neglect can be overcome. But healing first begins with further insight—insight into the ripple effect a father has on all the family relationships.

4

Your Father: More Than a Family Footnote

*G*ina, the second of four children, is a twenty-five-year-old university student who lives with her mother. Her parents divorced ten years ago but still talk occasionally. Her older sister and two younger brothers have moved out of the family home.

"He was so stern," she said of her father. "Irritable and stern. He would be annoyed with me over so many things. He was the principal in a nice private school, and he treated us like we were always late for class. After a while, he and Mom stopped fighting. I think they were just sick and tired of it all. Mom felt sorry for me and I felt sorry for her so we became very close—sort of best friends."

"How old were you?" I asked.

"About fifteen or so," she said. "I guess my mother and I were just disheartened by it all. I could never hurt her—she's been through so much. We still talk about my father sometimes. In fact, last night when I tucked her in, I . . ."

"Tucked who in?" I interrupted.

"My mother. I was sitting on the bed talking to her, and I was making her laugh because I kept making fun of my father's eccentric ways. We do this a lot. We laugh about the men in our lives."

Gina has had a number of boyfriends, mostly college students or guys she knew from her part-time job. They were fairly intense relationships in which she quickly fell deeply in love, yet it was never very long before the excitement began to die down. In retrospect, she recognizes a few of these as unwise relationships; she admits that she has a tendency to become involved with men who are already committed or otherwise unable to commit to her.

When asked why she dated these men, she said that she "hated being alone," without someone to care for her.

I asked her if her mother knew all the details of her romantic relationships.

"I tell her," Gina replied, "because I figure she'll know anyway."

"How would she know?"

"Come on, Dr. Schaller, she'd just know," she said, a smile playing across her face. "Mothers have a way of looking at you and knowing if you're in love, or tired, or holding a secret."

"Are you close to anyone other than your mother?"

"My brother Paul and I are very close." A thoughtful look came into her eyes. "I envy his independence. He's been out of the house for years. He's really the kind of person I'd like to be—independent and able to go for it and be a success."

Gina says she wants to be independent, yet she appears to be emotionally fused to her mother, even though she doesn't realize it. Although she envies her brother's life, she fears leaving her mother.

Inappropriate mother-child development is often induced by a distant or uninvolved father. Imagine a triangle made of string. The parents are at two corners and the child is at the third corner. What happens if you hook the father's corner and pull? The two corners that represent the mother and child are pulled together.

When a father is deceased, overworked, emotionally or physically absent, weak, hostile, or abusive, the children and their mother are often pulled together. They do not want to be left as emotional orphans, and sometimes in their attempts to avoid that, they may pull so close together that healthy parent/child boundaries are violated. One begins to wonder who is the parent and who is the child. The process of individualization (whereby a child becomes a respected, separate adult) becomes impaired.

Gina says she wants to move on, but she never does because of the separation it would cause between her and her mother. She tucks her mother into bed at night. In school, she has continually changed her major, "unintentionally" postponing her graduation. She says she wants to have her own life, but tells her mother absolutely everything in her life—her love interests, her dreams, her fears. And her mother seems to sabotage her daughter's moving out of the house by treating her daughter like an adolescent.

Gina is experiencing role confusion. It's great when adult children feel close to their parents, but the closeness should be based on a mature relationship between two adults. Gina's friendship with her mother is really a confused relationship in which she functions as her mother's "emotional husband."

Gina is a "good girl" who is trying to do the right thing. But her goodness is hurting her; both mother and child are trapped in a crippling relationship. Mother expects her child to kiss away the pain caused by her husband. Any attempts the daughter makes at disengagement are responded to with more pleas of need. If the child does not respond to this new plea, the mother may make the classic accusation, "You are selfish and only looking out for yourself." Gina has been made the emotional spouse and caretaker of her mother.

I have seen dozens of young adult children who are so busy caring for others that they have no time to care for themselves. They function as the third parent in the family. They have been taught not to think about themselves, because that would be selfish.

When a father deserts or neglects his appropriate role, the children tend to become either caretakers or scapegoats. The caretakers love their mothers in ways that are beyond the child's role; they may also function as eternal baby-sitters for their siblings. Occasionally, younger children look to their older brother or sister as the reliable "parent," because Mother is too emotionally crippled or just physically exhausted from playing both parental roles.

Scapegoats in the family are easy to identify. They are the ones getting into trouble in school, at work, or in their relationships. They may be called the black sheep of the family and the weight of that label often hurts them a great deal. In child psychiatry we sometimes see a young seven-year-old who is called "oppositional" and who is considered a "difficult child" by his parents. In other words, the parents come in upset because *the child* has a problem. In such cases one occasionally finds that the child is merely picking up the tension and hostility in the family and then acting out the family's anxious, hostile energy. The child is very sensitive to the family problems. The parents, however, often do not see their child as sensitive. They see him as difficult.

In Gina's family, Tom may be playing the role of the scapegoat. He is the only one who has not graduated from college and often drinks in excess. The reality is, however, that his problems started the year of his parents' divorce. Perhaps his behavior is a response to the problems he has perceived in his family.

What about the "independent gypsy"? In Gina's family Paul plays that role. She talks about missing her younger brother. "We used to go roller-skating together almost every week and we were both pretty good. We looked out for each other. We fought a lot, but we cared a lot, too. Now, though, he stays away from the family and avoids family gatherings. I'm lucky if I see him Thanksgiving and Christmas. He seems to feel that he doesn't fit in our family anymore. Even when he does stop by, he never stays more than two hours. In the past we used to argue a lot with my father and ignore my mother. Now that my father is gone, I thought I'd see Paul more, but nothing has changed."

Typically, withdrawn siblings like Gina's brother think of themselves as independent, but more thorough observation often reveals that they are hurt by their father experiences and are running away emotionally. Sometimes they look for "opposite families" and "opposite fathers"— families with qualities in stark contrast to their own. Unfortunately, because they avoid confronting and dealing with their family problems (confusing avoidance with independence), they continue to bear the pain of those problems. Gina rarely sees her brother because he has rejected not only his father, but the rest of the family as well.

Not everyone can identify with Gina's story; not everyone has been so handicapped by his or her father's influence. But we will discover, in the next chapter, the force of a father's impact on sexual identity and sexual expression.

5

The Father's Role in His Children's Sexual Identity

*V*ery young children are quite aware of their bodies and their sexuality.

Four-year-old girls do not need to read books by Gloria Steinem and Nancy Chodorow to help them feel good about being female. But they do pay particular attention to their father's reactions to their primitive "femininity," and they observe their father's responses to their mother's femininity. When a little girl is ignored, sees her mother mistreated, or sees her brothers get all the attention, she might feel that she'd be better off if she were a boy.

Carol felt that way. She was raised in a strongly patriarchal Italian household. As a young girl, she had made desperate attempts to be close to her father, whom she loved and admired. This man had a great love of fishing, and went at least once a month, usually taking Carol's two older brothers along.

Preparation for those trips was always a dramatic ritual that involved the whole family. Her father and brothers would get the canoe down from the garage rafters, Dad would carefully check the lures, and Carol and her mother would pack the food and whatever else the "men" were going to need. Carol remembers asking her father, "Daddy, can I put the pillow in the car for you?" It never seemed to occur to him that she was begging to go.

One morning, after completing the packing ritual the evening before, Carol was awakened by the sound of her brothers noisily "being quiet" as they went down the stairs. Each was telling the other to stop making so much noise. Carol was swept up in the excitement as she heard them thumping down the stairs, and hurriedly went down after them as if it were Christmas morning.

Yet when she reached the bottom, she began to feel sad and empty. The sadness increased as she watched her father and eldest brother place the last of the perishables in the cooler. She wanted to be taken along, but knew it was useless. Her father waved good-bye and told her to get back to bed, and she silently and tearfully watched them pull out of the driveway on their way to adventure.

Carol shook her head as she related that sad occasion to me. "That's when I started to feel there was something wrong with me, that I wasn't quite right."

I encouraged her to continue.

"I didn't realize it then, but I suppose I felt that being a girl was bad . . . second class . . . defective. I just wanted to be with him, you know. Even when I tried to hug him and sit on his lap, he would become very uncomfortable. He just didn't know how to relate to a girl."

"How do you think that affected you?"

"I became a real tomboy. If it was girlish, I avoided it. I still have scars on my knees because I was into sports and did a lot of dangerous things."

"Did that make your dad notice you? Did he ever take you fishing?"

"No." After a long pause she said it again. "No. He never took me fishing."

Unfortunately for some daughters, the things Dad enjoys are "men's things." For many traditional fathers there is a clear dividing line between men's activities and women's activities, and that left a wall between Carol and her father. He was not interested in doing activities that she liked, and she was not allowed to join him in male adventures. The take-home message for Carol was that to be a woman was to be rejected—it was of lesser value.

Another way an unhealthy father-daughter relationship can affect a woman's sexuality is to bring on a preoccupation with her appearance that may result in compulsive exercise, compulsive eating, or dieting and eating disorders. In the past, severe forms of eating disorders have been associated in psychological theory with problems in the mother-daughter bond. Yet Margo Maine, the senior editor of *Eating Disorders: The Journal of Treatment and Prevention,* says she has been surprised to realize the large role of the father in eating and body identity problems. Maine describes her meetings with a fifteen-year-old named Barbara who was hospitalized for anorexia and bulimia treatment.[1]

Barbara was beautiful, shy, and terribly emaciated. After some time in therapy, she gradually began to speak of feelings of hopelessness regarding her parents' marriage, and particularly regarding her father. She had been in outpatient treatment for a year and had made very little progress, so Maine decided to pursue the girl's "father issues."[2]

Eventually, Barbara's desire for closeness with her father became clear. "She thought that having a different body would please him, so she dieted, lost weight, overexercised, and purged, masking her pain and emptiness."[3]

Thankfully, her father was willing to help Barbara. He was concerned about his daughter, but didn't know how to show it.

> He only knew how to buy her things, hoping she would be happy again. He did not know to give of himself because he had never been shown how. Lucky for Barbara he was willing to learn. Through family therapy, he became emotionally expressive and more actively involved in Barbara's life. The changes he made helped her to recover.[4]

Hearing about Carol and Barbara, one might expect that boys would have less trouble with their sexual identity. At least they would be the ones taken on fishing trips and other "manly" outings, right? But what if you were a boy who didn't like fishing or sports? What if you were a boy like Peter?

Peter's dad knew all the football teams, their win/loss records, and their players' names. He could describe—at great length—all the big plays of the last twenty years. He always had season tickets. While the man had never played pro ball himself, he had achieved some success in college sports.

When Peter was born, his father naturally hoped his son would share his enthusiasm for sports. Little Peter soon found a baseball glove on his hand and a football under the Christmas tree. While the boy liked being with his father, he just never developed an interest in football or baseball.

Peter's mother had a love of learning and, early on, she exposed her son to many different types of writers. This was it! Peter loved to read. He would escape to the world of fantasy and adventure as often as he could. Books brought Peter a world of wonder and delight, but his father ignored his passion. Once, while Peter was a young adolescent, his father invited him to go to a game by saying, "Why don't you put that wimpy book down and go to the game."

Peter got his father's message: a boy who read "wimpy books" was a "wimpy son." He understood that his father doubted his masculinity. In the mind of Peter's father, women read and men played sports, and real men vehemently rejected anything that smacked of femininity.[5] Because of his father's influence, Peter grew up wondering if he were weird or homosexual. His father's constricted definition of maleness profoundly affected Peter's sexual identity.

I remember many other cases in which both young men and women wrestled with feelings of unattractiveness and even feelings of self-loathing that were brought on at least in part by comments made by their fathers. Over and over I have heard men and women sadly recall the "affectionate" names they were given by naive fathers—names like "fats" and "my little pig"—names that wounded deeply and scarred permanently.

How Sex Is Affected by Father Troubles

Whether you realize it or not, your view of sex is probably affected in some way by your relationship with your father. Whether you have an impulsive sexuality, a healthy sexual appetite, or no sexual appetite at all, your dad has probably influenced your sex life.

Joan was a single woman working as a secretary in a law firm. She had come to me for counseling because she was concerned over her lack of interest in sex. She worried that something was wrong with her. She wondered if she were meant to be single. After some discussion it became clear that her diminished interest in sex wasn't so much a "gift for singleness" as it was a consequence of extreme childhood pressures.

Joan was the eldest of five children. She had mixed memories of her childhood, "some good and some bad," as she described it. The major bad event was the death of her mother when she was an adolescent. Joan became something of an administrator after her mother's death, looking after her younger siblings and her mourning father. She made sure he was eating well and paying the bills. He regularly expected her to fill her mother's shoes by asking her to do much of what her mother had done, despite the fact that she was only an adolescent. In our sessions, she repeatedly told long and detailed stories about her brothers and sisters, as if they were my patients instead of her.

She had been overwhelmed with playing the "mother and wife role," and withdrew from the intensity of the responsibility. Sexual interest and dating would have meant another "wife" and "mother" role and more overwhelming family responsibilities. Often when a child or adolescent is expected to shoulder adult responsibilities, she will either ascend to amazing heights or withdraw in fear and anxiety. Joan was in the latter category.

While Joan could "take it or leave it" when it came to men and romance, not all women respond in the same manner when they suffer from father hunger. Diane responded quite differently. That was evident almost from the moment she walked through the door into my office. Did I say walked? Sashayed would be more like it—in a rather seductive dress, too. Diane's conversations included occasional playful sexual innuendos, and she told me that she had had a number of romantic relationships since her adolescence.

Diane's passion for dating began not long after her father's departure. Her parents had divorced primarily because her father was having an affair, and Diane stayed in the custody of her mother. During our counseling it became clear that Diane had probably gained a number of messages from her father's departure, two of the most important being "Dad left, so I better try harder next time to keep him," and "Men leave you when they stop liking you."

Diane had a father-void that she was attempting to fill with seductiveness toward her male peers, older males, or authority figures. Having "lost" her father once, she was now in search of him in peer relationships, acting out sexually in an attempt to find father love.

In his book, *Father, the Figure and the Force,* Christopher Andersen quotes a study of 7,000 women who were working in topless bars and strip clubs. That study found that the majority of these women came from fatherless homes.[6] While their career choices were most likely driven partly by economic motivations, Andersen reports, "Most of the women conceded that in baring their bodies to strangers they were probably looking for the male attention they had never gotten during their childhood. Lacking that foundation, many of these women admitted that they did not rely on men for intimacy. Of the 7,000 women interviewed for the study, half turned out to be lesbians."[7]

Andersen implies that a fatherless woman's longing for male attention does not necessarily mean she will believe men are safe enough for sexual intimacy. He also seems to imply that homosexuality in these women was related to their alienation from their fathers. Could this be true? Is homosexuality no more than a cry for fathering? Is that why half of these fatherless women were lesbians?

In the past century there have been many theories put forth for the causes of homosexuality, including genetic and hormonal abnormalities and environmental factors. Some experts offer evidence for all of these positions, and I do not intend to posit that "fathers cause homosexuality." However, some psychological researchers strongly suggest that father hunger can promote the development of homosexual tendencies.

Dr. George Reker, who has done extensive research on male homosexuality, concludes:

> The fathers of homosexual sons are reported to be less affectionate than fathers of heterosexual sons. In one study of forty homosexual men, there was not a single case in which the man reported having had an affectionate relationship with his father. In fact, homosexual men often hate and even fear their fathers. . . .
>
> The fathers of homosexual sons are most often described as being aloof, hostile and rejecting. More than four-fifths of adult male homosexuals report that their fathers were physically or psychologically absent from their homes while growing up. . . .

Significantly, only 13 percent of the homosexuals in a controlled study identified with their fathers in comparison to 66 percent of the heterosexual men in the same study.[8]

While the causes of male homosexuality may be more complex than the single influence of father deprivation, my own experience working with homosexual men has supported Dr. Reker's findings. In every case, the father relationship was problematic, and without exception these men have described their fathers as absent, hostile, harsh, weak, cold, or indifferent. While most of these homosexual men were entirely masculine in their demeanor, those with feminine "body language" typically had mothers who were overinvolved in their sons' treatment with me. They would call regularly to ask how their sons were doing.

One of these men was a twenty-five-year-old named Roger. He was stocky and broad-shouldered, with a kind heart and a constant smile. He was the kind of guy who could make you feel comfortable or nervous—depending on how he looked at you. You wouldn't have wanted to get on his bad side, because he was tough. Thankfully, I stayed on his good side.

His earliest father memories had to do with his parents fighting, and one particular fight stood out in his mind. His parents had been arguing and his father angrily stomped out of the house. When he returned a few hours later, he found that his wife had locked the door. As his father pounded on the door in anger, Roger clung to his mother's dress in fear. Finally, his father kicked in the door, stormed into the house, and began beating Roger's mother; he threw her into the fireplace wall and began hitting her again and again with his fists. Roger, who was only four, rushed out from behind the chair where he had been hiding in an attempt to defend his mother.

He screamed for his father to stop, and when he was ignored, he ran over and bit the man's leg. His reward was to be included in his father's attack. Roger dates this incident as the start of his hatred toward his father.

The couple promptly divorced, and the boy and his mother moved several times before they finally moved in with Roger's maternal grandparents. But then one day, about two years later, his father showed up and demanded custody of the boy. His former wife refused and tried to call the police, but his father attacked her again, and dragged a tearful, struggling Roger to his car. Roger never did get to say good-bye to his mother (or his grandmother, who died soon afterward).

Despite his father's desperate efforts to get custody of him, it was perfectly clear to Roger that his father had no real love for him.

"My father didn't really want me," he said. "He just didn't want me to be with my mother. He dropped me off at his parents and took off for another two years. When he returned, he introduced me to my 'new mother' and told me I was leaving to go live with him. When I cried because I was going to miss my grandparents, he called me a sissy. He would often take me to work at his gas station. And while we were there he would tell me not to speak unless I was spoken to; I should be seen and not heard, he said. If I made a mistake he would smack me and make me sit in the car."

It was around this time that Roger's sixteen-year-old cousin, Thomas, began making sexual advances toward him. Roger was only eight, full of hurt and confusion, and he accepted his cousin's advances because "I thought this was love," he said. "From then on I was attracted to the 'love' of men."

While your relationship with your father can and does affect your sexuality (not only negatively, as it did for Roger and Diane, but also positively), it doesn't mean you *have* to be any certain way. If you believe your expression of your sexual nature is unhealthy and alienating, it need not remain that way. But healthy change will often not occur until you understand why you are the way you are. That is true not only of your sexuality, but also of your marriage and your career.

6

Fathers and Love Relationships

. . . .

*B*ecky's marriage fell apart after twelve years, and when it did, she asked herself all the usual questions: "What went wrong?" "What didn't I see?" "What do I need to change in order to prevent another failed relationship?"

She was surprised to note that after her divorce she felt like an adolescent again. Irritations with her family resurfaced now that there was no spouse to buffet them.

As she reflected on her family and her past, she came to believe that her road to marriage—and divorce—had been paved not merely by her father, but even earlier, by her paternal grandfather.

Becky's grandfather was an emotionally distant alcoholic who set the tone for her father's entire family. Becky's father was determined that he would not be the sort of father his own dad had been, and he wasn't. He rarely drank, he was involved in all the daily affairs of his three children, and he never talked about his problems. He was not what one would call a passionate, emotional man. His emotions were stuffed deep down.

Becky loved her father, but when she reached her late teens she began to feel constricted, because he wanted to be involved in every aspect of her life. The involvement and attention she had loved so much as a young child became unpleasant to a young woman struggling to achieve independence and self-determination. Becky felt as if her father and the "family clan" were too close to her, so she went hundreds of miles away to attend college.

That's where she met Peter, a free-spirited and independent political science major. He was so different from her father—full of emotion and passion, and yet quite willing to let her "do her own thing." She liked many things about Peter, especially the way he supported her independence. Peter, in contrast to her father, was only too happy to give her space, because space was all he had ever known in his own family.

Once they were married, however, Becky began to resent Peter's distance. "He acted as if he couldn't care less if we talked or ignored each other," she said. "It became very frustrating."

Peter's father was not at all like Becky's dad. In fact, among Peter's most vivid memories of his father were the oft-repeated words, "Just remember, when you're eighteen, you're on your own!" Becky and Peter found in each other an escape from their family trials, particularly their father difficulties. But that was not the foundation upon which to build a lasting marriage. Unfortunately, the couple waited until things had crumbled almost to dust—until there was little to put back together—before seeking professional help with their problems.

Becky's story illustrates a principle in marriage choice. Fathers are generally the male template from which marriages, especially early marriages, are chosen. Some women, like Sophia Loren, admit to marrying a father substitute. Others purposefully seek out and marry someone who is the exact opposite of their fathers.

Josephine was twenty-five when she learned that her parents were divorcing after thirty years of marriage. The news sent shock waves through the entire family. She spent hours discussing the situation with her younger brother and two older sisters. What had happened was clear: Her father had started having an affair with one of his employees, a woman ten years his junior. He had asked his wife for a divorce and was willing to make a "fair" settlement to ensure that she was "taken care of."

Until then, Josephine had rarely dated; she wasn't that interested. Yet she was married within ten months of finding out about her father's affair. In retrospect, she believes that her father "died" to her when he divorced her mother, leaving her with a huge loss. She hungered for a faithful man, a man who would be a reliable male connection, and she sought to find that connection in a husband.

Josephine's choice of a husband was also interesting. Her previous dates had all been with leaders of various groups, guys who were "well liked" and motivated in school or in their work. Yet she married a very different type.

Jason was a man who needed quite a bit of support to function, freely describing himself as "fairly needy." Jason would be unlikely to leave a marriage, but not necessarily because of faithfulness or commitment; he would stay because he needed the relationship in order to feel good about himself.

The timing of Josephine's marriage was related to the loss of her respected father; her choice of a partner was influenced by her need to have a husband who would never leave her, who would not hurt her as her father had done. Josephine's marriage did not necessarily resolve her pain over the divorce. It may have short-circuited the process of resolving the pain of her father's "abandonment." Josephine did not face the pain of her father's betrayal, and may even have invited more pain by the way she reacted to her father's influence. She picked marriage as a solution to her wounded heart. In effect, her father's affair largely controlled the most important relationship of her life.

Fathers and the *Real* World of Work

Fathers not only influence their children's marriages; they also affect their career choices and success.

My father gave me freedom to follow my own career goals. He told me to choose my own path even though he silently worried over my decisions. When I studied religion, a very poor money-maker, he did not oppose me. When I worked (virtually for pennies) in a religious rehabilitation center, he did not oppose me. Yet I heard another message, too.

My father was an extremely gifted student during all of his schooling, and even though he did not talk about it, family friends told me he was legendary. I even had a college physics professor approach me once, out of the blue, and say, "James, your father was the most intelligent man to ever come to this school. He was amazing." Well, of course I was proud of his ability and my association with him, especially because I could always say I had his genes. But I was also intimidated.

I realize now that I internalized his academic success as the gold standard. His achievements were partly my goals—the things I wanted to shoot for. But straight A's and academic honors in pre-med are very high goals.

My father also had the habit, during arguments, of using quotes from "experts," people who were the "greatest in their fields." While this is common in verbal debates, I got the message that true persons of value were those who were experts at something and great in their fields. Today, I am one of the few psychiatrists in this country with two degrees in theology, and though there are many legitimate reasons for my vocational choice, I believe part of my motivation was a need to feel valued through playing the role of the "expert."

While my father's impact on my choice of a profession was unintentional, it was still influential. Such influence is often more coercive—and destructive. I heard about a man who graduated from an Ivy League medical school and, upon receiving his medical degree, threw it at his father. "Here's *your* degree," he said with a sneer. Then he went out and became a musician. That young man obviously felt controlled and manipulated into obtaining a medical degree.

It is nothing new to suggest that fathers often view their children as narcissistic extensions of themselves. We have all seen the sports father who wants to find his own success through his son's prowess on the playing field. I have heard a few pastors talking about the Christian vocation their children will pursue—sometimes even while those children are still in diapers. Such behavior, conscious or not, is terribly presumptuous and destructive.

Nathan came to me because he couldn't seem to keep a job; he was always finding some reason to quit. Because of this, and because he could find nothing more than part-time work for months at a time, he was deeply in debt. He was a pleasant, brawny man in his mid-thirties. He was the youngest of four children and the only male in his family. He revered his mother as a "saint" and endured his father.

Nathan was always borrowing money to cover debts, and then could not repay what he had borrowed. He did this with two girlfriends, both of whom eventually left him. One said, "I was tired of trying to mother and motivate him."

Nathan's father was a successful salesman for an industrial machine company (despite his drinking problem). He would regularly put Nathan down and criticize him for his "incompetence" and "laziness." His favorite nickname for his son was "Pea-brain." He tried to motivate his son by insulting him, but he succeeded only in making Nathan feel like a failure.

As a result, Nathan retreated into fantasies such as running a country inn in an idyllic setting. He had lost in the competitive game of life so severely that he preferred wishing to trying.

Some, like Nathan, give up on their work; others, like Jill, go to the other extreme. It became apparent to me in my sessions with Jill that her career was largely controlled by father issues.

Jill's father was a fireman who also worked a second job. When he came home at night he was tired, irritable, and quick to isolate himself to avoid his daughter. Jill remembered that she was a fairly hyper child with a tendency to be disobedient. Her fatigued and frustrated mother would often respond to Jill's antics by saying, "Now you've done it! When your father gets home you'll get it good." Her father would come in late at night, be told the bad news, and then smack a child he never really knew.

As a child and adolescent, Jill remembers her father was emotionally removed. When he wasn't smacking his two kids, he was withdrawn and watching TV, out with his friends, or sleeping. He had little affirmation to offer his daughter. For many years, in many different ways, Jill asked her father, "Do you like me?" But she never got the answer she wanted, so now she looks for her boss to give it. She's knocking herself out to gain respect from a man who's only too willing to let her work as hard as she wants. After all, the more she accomplishes under his direction, the better he looks to his superiors.

Jill's loyalty to this boss has actually hurt, rather than helped, her career. Last year a family friend tried to help her get a much better job—more pay, better benefits, paid college tuition, and half the commute time. Jill wasn't even interested in checking it out; she felt that even considering it would be "disloyal."

Jill's boss is hardly interested in being Jill's surrogate father; he has a payroll to meet and, to him, that's the bottom line. No matter how hard she works, Jill's boss won't be able to supply what she's looking for—because he's not her father.

What Is Your Definition of "Normal"?

Not only do fathers affect their children's marital and vocational decisions and actions, they also help their children define what is normal and what is not. Fatherly standards of normalcy are learned over the course of hundreds of thousands of interactions between children and their fathers.

Let's take just a moment to look at a sample of some of the messages about "normalcy" that fathers might pass on to their children:

- Feelings are dangerous. If you examine them you might explode and die. In the home it's important to keep your feelings hidden.
- Chaos is normal and okay. We may yell and threaten, but be of good cheer because this is normal.
- People are to be used to obtain things. It is okay to violate someone else's boundaries in order to have your own needs met.
- We are the special family. We are better than others.
- We are the pitiable and downtrodden family.
- People in this family have specific allegiances to a church, a political party, and a sports team. We also dislike the same relatives and ethnic groups. If you deviate from this you are a betrayer and don't love your father or our family.
- In relationships, it is important to show that you don't need anyone. It is okay to enjoy them, but just don't act as if you need people. If you must be with people, make it look almost accidental and incidental. It is best to be as independent as possible.
- Women are in charge of relationships. They make the phone calls to arrange outings. They call the children to say hello. Fathers are not supposed to be nurturing.
- Men are to be feared and avoided. You can be emotionally close only to a woman.
- If you're not the winner, don't bother playing the game.

- Manhood is something you achieve. One is not simply born male; you must prove your manhood through exploits. Men are strong and in control.
- Men must show their hurt with anger. Women must communicate their anger with tears. If a man cries, he is effeminate and weak.
- If a wife works, that means her husband must be a poor provider.
- Children should be just like their parents. They should fulfill the hopes and dreams of their parents.
- Men should treat women in a paternalistic manner and use them to achieve their ends.

How many of the above ideas did your father communicate to you? To what extent has that—and other messages not listed above—defined what you consider to be "normal"? It is not hard to see how such ideas shape us. It is possible, however, to overcome those messages, but they must be identified and addressed before they can be healed.

Having looked at a father's role in our definition of normalcy, it would be useful to turn our attention to a somewhat related question: What are normal or common feelings for those with father deficiency?

Perhaps the most intriguing place to look for an answer to this question is in the lives of those with severe father deficiency—orphans. In my opinion, the more you experience father deficiency, the more you are prone to orphan-like feelings.

Part 2

Orphan Psychology

7

Shining the Light on Orphan Psychology

· ·

S ome ancient cultures were more accurate about father issues than some of our present-day cultures. For example, if a child's father died, the child was simply called an orphan. These cultures probably believed a fatherless child's emotional life would resemble the life of a child with neither father nor mother. But is it only those with a deceased father who have orphan-like emotions? No!

Sometimes I think and feel very much like a fatherless child—even though both of my parents are still alive.[1]

I remember lying in bed one evening a number of years ago, wrestling with many old emotional pains and worrying about my finances. So what did I do? I called my father. He had always been a man you could depend on—the consistent, reliable oak (and it didn't hurt that he could lend you money in a pinch).

It was just about midnight. He happened to be emptying the dishwasher by the kitchen phone when I called, and we were able to talk for about thirty minutes. But it was a very different conversation from our previous ones.

After I talked about my fears and trials, he began to discuss his own fears and trials. I suspect that he was attempting to talk to his son as an adult to an adult. He did not pretend to be an invincible oak; he wanted a time of mutual sharing.

While I enjoyed the intimacy and the privilege of hearing more of his personal side, I was also unsettled. I realized that night how utterly finite and weak all fathers are. As we become adults, we realize that they are not mighty oaks; they often bow under life's pressures like the smallest sapling. Their health and strength are entirely transient. Part of me tasted the orphan's life that night, and it was a bitter sip. I felt very much alone, and vulnerable.

Orphan emotions may occur even in a person who has two parents, because orphan emotions are based on psychological experience, not necessarily whether your parents are alive. For example, orphan feelings have to do with the realization of the limitations of parents—were they able to listen without distraction, care deeply and personally, protect, and soothe loneliness? Most of us have several orphan triggers that are most obvious in times of crisis. Stress has a way of revealing triggers that would otherwise remain hidden. Stress often reveals the "real you"—the orphan core.

Stop right now and take a mental snapshot of yourself. Look at your fantasies, your dreams, and your deepest feelings and motives. If you have trouble getting a clear picture, ask yourself some questions like these: When you let your mind wander, where does it go? What fantasy dialogues take place? What images appear? What emotions arise? What makes you irritated or afraid? What would your loved ones say motivates and controls you the most?

Remember, though, that it often takes a very long time to gain insight into our deeper, more primitive orphan feelings. Some that I've discovered in myself took a decade or more to find.

Here is a sampling of some possible orphan feelings, thoughts, beliefs, and concerns. How many apply to you?

- When push comes to shove, no one will help me but me.
- When someone is thoughtful to me, it surprises me.
- I think a lot about losing the ones I love.
- I relate to underdogs because I feel like one.
- When I love someone or something it dies or leaves me.
- I often find the world to be intimidating and scary.

- I feel vulnerable, especially financially.
- I have vivid memories of times when I had no one to depend on.
- My friends mean more to me than my parents.
- I tend to see things in black and white.
- People say I am too intense in my relationships.
- I feel closer to animals than to people.
- I often feel indifferent or bored in my relationships.
- I realize that I am often far too critical.
- If I were to draw a picture of what my life looks like, I would be alone in the picture.
- I need a lot of reassurance.
- I find myself wanting people to hold and baby me.
- I love getting advice and receiving attention from an authority figure.
- I tend to feel more cynical about authority than most people.
- When someone withdraws from me, I get angry or afraid and pursue them too zealously.
- Intimacy often equals pain for me.
- I am uncomfortable asserting myself—for any reason.
- I regularly feel like people are trying to take advantage of me.
- I believe that closeness is a prelude to loss.
- Projects are more important to me than people.
- Sometimes I feel that people are interchangeable; it's fairly easy for me to change significant people in my life.
- I am beginning to see that most of what I have called "love" is really disguised need.
- I often wonder who will care for me if I become ill.
- Generally, I am restless and insecure.
- I use unhealthy ways to nurture myself, as if there is a very deep void inside of me.
- I feel safe when my world is ordered and uncomfortable when things are out of line.
- I am very aggressive in my work.
- I feel unprotected when I travel or when I am home alone.
- I prefer fantasy to reality.
- Whenever I am criticized, it hurts me and I replay the incident in my mind for days afterward.
- I have just relocated and don't have a good support network yet.

- I have recently been separated or divorced and I feel cut off from everyone.
- I often feel as if I'm totally depleted—that I have nothing more to give.
- God seems far away much of the time.
- I don't really enjoy praying, even though I do it.
- I hate being the center of attention. It makes me uncomfortable.
- When someone really listens to me, I am taken by the novelty of the experience.
- Sometimes I feel that people will find out I am not worthy of their friendship and withdraw from me.
- When I do something wrong, I find it hard to think about God.
- I have the capacity to be very reactive—as if there is anger stored away just waiting for a slight.
- People only pretend to care; they really don't.
- I am suspicious of nonreligious people.
- The world is a very tough place.

These are but a few of what I call "orphan emotions," core beliefs that can be typical of an orphan mentality. Such thoughts and feelings may occasionally afflict people with good parents, but they will be especially pronounced among those who suffer from father hunger. Let me explain.

If a person has a negative relationship with his father (or none at all), we might say he is "half an orphan." The many gifts and psychological reinforcements that a father would give are gone. For example, he may have rarely tucked you in, kissed you, wrestled with you, danced with you, or shared a game of catch with you. He did not offer praise for a chore well done, a new outfit, a well-caught fly ball, a college degree, or some other achievement. A child seeking the protection from a distant father is left feeling undefended. And if a father is dead, absent, or unable to provide support, his children may live in poverty and loneliness. Single mothers often have less education and fewer marketable skills. The loss of a father may mean that Mom must work, increasing the child's sense of abandonment.

Having a father void under any of these circumstances can leave a child with definite orphan feelings or beliefs. It is possible to feel cut off and alone, even in a home that still has a mother. Such a child can feel isolated and troubled, and may not know for decades how profoundly the loss of the father connection has hurt him.

Some fathers deplete rather than give. A father who beats, molests, verbally degrades, disrupts the stability of the home by his alcohol, gambling, drugs, or moodiness is an *anti-father*. He sucks the life from the veins of his family; he functions as an emotional black hole. He steals the carefree laughter of childhood. Such a father produces a large amount of psychic orphanhood in his children, forcing them to function as emotional orphans, even though both parents are still alive.

A father is not always the only parent with problems; a father's severe dysfunction may be a sign that the mother also has problems. In my experience, many children aren't as quick to see their mothers' shortcomings as they are the shortcomings of their fathers.

June realized this five years after her parents divorced. She had always been closer to her mother while she was growing up, and this continued after her parents divorced. However, after her first child was born she began to see certain things in her mother. She noticed that her mother's gifts always had certain unspoken expectations and demands associated with them, such as, "Sure I'll baby-sit, but that means I may stop in whenever I feel like it."

June became most annoyed by the way her mother used guilt to manipulate her, and the way she sometimes acted childish, asking for help with things that any adult should be able to do. Slowly, June came to see that both of her parents had serious psychological barriers to maturity. But that revelation did not assuage her orphan feelings; it intensified them. Before, she felt she could at least depend on Mom; when she realized that even her mother had serious issues to overcome, she felt more alone.

The truth is that even children from good homes, where there are two mature parents, can experience orphan feelings. Why? Because mothers and fathers are really only grown children themselves, mere humans whose heads are filled with their own problems and fears. For example, the father who comes home from his construction job after twelve hours may not have enough energy to play games with his little girl, no matter how much he loves her, which may cause the child to feel somewhat abandoned.

Moreover, because every father is typically much older than his son or daughter, adult children often feel like orphans in their parents' later years. It can be shocking to watch your father's hair begin to gray, to see his health start to fail, and to read the names of his peers on the obituary page.

I remember the shock I felt each time a close friend of my father's died. Their deaths made me realize that my father's life was ticking away, and I was frightened. When he had a permanently disabling heart attack seven years later, these feelings emerged again. We all face the orphan experience; some earlier, some later.

Lessons from Animals and Orphans

Beginning in recent centuries with the great eighteenth-century classifier, Linnaeus,[2] researchers have compiled dozens of accounts of children raised by animals during the past four hundred years. While not all of the stories are rigorously documented, some have been carefully recorded and debated. These extreme cases show orphans worthy of profound pity. But their trials may help teach us about our own subtle orphan feelings, perhaps offering insight about our own perspectives and perceptions.[3]

Probably the most reliable case comes from the Indian missionary, J. A. Singh. This case was carefully and thoroughly investigated by A. Gesell and Robert Zingg,[4] the latter being professor of anthropology at the University of Denver. The major facts are as follows:

> While visiting [a] village not far from Midnapore, Singh heard reports of a strange "human spirit" running with a pack of wolves that was terrorizing the countryside. On investigation he observed in front of the wolf's den two creatures in company with three large wolves and two cubs. When an attempt was made to capture these creatures, two adult wolves escaped, and the she-wolf who was defending the cubs was killed. The two "wolf children" and two cubs in the den were captured.
>
> The younger child was a girl (Amala) about eighteen months old, the older a girl (Kamala) about eight years old. [According to Gesell, they had made a] thorough adaptation to the wolf's den.[5]

Kamala was thoroughly wolf-like, and the details of her life were recorded in the diary of Reverend Singh. She ran incredibly fast on all fours, and had huge calluses on her knees, the soles of her feet, her elbows, and her palms. She was most comfortable naked and felt no shame in this state until after years of human socialization. At first, she would eat only raw meat and lapped liquid out of a bowl, crouched on all fours.[6]

The girls were taken to Singh's Midnapore orphanage, where they confronted—and presented—many challenges. Kamala was so frightened by people that she growled and bared her teeth threateningly, occasionally even biting other children who approached her. Yet she shared her food with the orphanage dogs. In fact, Kamala preferred the company of cats or chickens over human company.[7]

Both girls demonstrated a superior sense of sight, smell, and hearing, and were able to withstand extremes of hot or cold temperature. Neither child showed any humor; neither smiled while at the orphanage. When Amala, the younger child, died after one year in captivity, Kamala slowly (apparently reluctantly at first) began to make efforts to become close to other humans. But she did not experience mature relational closeness, nor did she marry.[8]

Kamala's psychology is striking. She had problems with intimacy, preferring animals and isolation to human contact. She was very comfortable with abusive situations—temperature extremes did not affect her. Why? It appears that abusive temperature extremes were merely business as usual for her. She was highly vigilant; she had learned, in a world full of hunters and carnivores, never to relax. She was also intensely serious; she never laughed. Kamala also shows us that orphan rules or patterns are hard to break; she lapped milk and ran like a dog for a long time after entering human society.

Kamala's experiences offer extreme illustrations of or metaphors for our own orphan feelings.

Another interesting case concerns a youth known as the Wild Boy of Aveyron. Itard, a leading French educator and the man who became his tutor, gives this account:

> [He was a] child of eleven or twelve, who . . . years before had been seen completely naked in the Caune Woods seeking acorns and roots to eat.

... [Years later he was] met in the same place in ... 1799 by three sportsmen who seized him as he was climbing into a tree to escape from their pursuit. Conducted to a neighboring hamlet . . . he broke loose . . . and gained the mountains, where he wandered during the most rigorous winter weather, draped rather than covered with a tattered shirt.

[Eventually] he was retaken, watched and cared for . . . [in] the hospital of Saint-Afrique. . . . He remained equally wild and shy, impatient and restless. [And after a few months] orders were given that the child should be brought to Paris. . . .

[In Paris, he appeared as] a disgustingly dirty child . . . who bit and scratched those who opposed him, who showed no affection for those who attended him; and who was in short, indifferent to everything and attentive to nothing.[9]

The boy spent nine years with Itard, who was entirely committed to the child and referred to him as "Victor." Itard estimated that Victor had probably been in the wilds since the age of four. Since the child was naked and fleeing the approach of men at the age of eleven or so, and had been seen in the woods several years prior to that, Itard assumed that he was already accustomed to living alone, and that he had been wild for years.[10]

Itard goes on to highlight a few of the boy's unusual characteristics. He was able to break relational bonds with indifference. After the boy was captured, a poor peasant man had welcomed and cared for him, lavishing upon him "all the tokens of a father's love," yet Victor thought nothing of leaving him.[11]

Itard also writes that Victor was unable to offer acts of true sacrifice and service. As soon as he was done with a meal and his needs were satisfied, he no longer wanted anything to do with any other human being. Indeed, even his caresses "were no less self-interested," because his touch was only a means to gain the satisfaction of his own desires and wants. Itard concludes that Victor was "insensible to every kind of moral influence," with "an insurmountable aversion to society."[12]

Though Victor's orphan experience is similar to Kamala's, he also offers us some additional insights. Like Kamala, Victor was very much afraid of human relationships, preferring a cold winter in the wild mountains alone to warmth with humans. Intimacy seemed to represent a sort of death to him. When Victor met men in the woods he assumed they were his enemies, and even regarded the fatherly French peasant who cared for him as unimportant. Itard makes it clear that Victor's later inter-actions with people were solely motivated by a desire to meet his needs. Victor gave nothing, but was like a hungry child crying at the breast of his mother, caring not at all about his mother's weariness. And finally, Victor had one clear moral code—to survive and be cared for at all costs.

In their summary of these cases of profound isolation from humans, Langmeier and Matejcek conclude that these children were very much afraid of human intimacy. Their later relationships were unstable and characterized by an intense need to please and submit in order to meet their insatiable demands for love and attention. Sexual behavior was auto-erotic, poorly controlled, and was not rooted in caring relationships. Orphans such as these also desire intense stimulation and have poor frus-tration tolerance.[13] To these observations we should add the obvious, that early on the children took on the qualities of whomever or what-ever gave them a shred of affection and attention—even if it was a wolf offering to nurse them!

These cases, though they are obviously extreme, perhaps reveal some of our own fears about life, and hint at some of the orphan feelings we may have.

First, we noted that the two orphans, Kamala and Victor, were both casual about intimacy. In fact, at their core they feared human closeness. Even after the loss of her sister, Kamala was very slow to develop a rela-tionship with her human caretakers. Victor was also content to leave his caretaker and surrogate father when he left for Paris.

Studies done on children who have been exposed to impaired par-enting have shown that there are a number of reactions to orphan sen-sations. Some of these reactions are evident immediately, but others may not emerge until years later.

Some children withdraw into a secret inner world to restore them-selves. They use extensive fantasy, or attempt self-nurture by anything that will affect the body, such as drugs, massages, trips to the doctor, and isolated rest. Others aggressively reach outward, seeking pleasure through the senses. They seek to gain nurture through food, music or movie bingeing, masturbation or other sexual experiences, aggressive work, and buying sprees. They turn to such things when they feel cut off in their key relationships, behaving like abandoned infants who rage because they are left alone and empty.[14]

Such people fear true intimacy because, after all, if you've been hurt once, it's possible you could be hurt again—and that's a risk you don't want to take.

Michele is that way. Her father was physically abusive to her, beginning when she was a tiny child. As an adult, she says she does not fear intimacy, but she has no deep relationships with men. When she first came to see me, she confessed that she would have preferred to be counseled by a woman. Why? Therapy can be a form of intimacy, and Michele was uncomfortable with any sort of intimacy with a man. The professional boundaries around our sessions are not protective enough for her. Even though she is in the midst of a crisis and needs to see me every week, she prefers seeing me only twice a month; more often would be "too intense," she says.

Michele is quite clear that her reluctance to see me more often is not because of any expense related to the sessions, but simply because I am a male. And, because she reacts that way to me, it's likely that she is avoiding emotional closeness with other men, too.

Iris's father was an airline pilot when she was growing up; he was gone most of the time. In fact, Iris says she never really knew him. Presently, she is engaged to be married for the second time, and says defensively that she is in no hurry to get married (even though she quickly set her wedding date before any sort of premarital counseling could be set up).

Iris has an orphan's view of intimacy; she views intimacy as a fragile and unstable connection. She perceives closeness as a thing to grab quickly, perhaps because Daddy will be flying away again soon. She cannot entertain the belief that intimacy grows slowly, like a tree, and is the fruit of gradual and proven consistency, because she has never experienced that type of relationship with any man.

When Iris's boyfriend wants to be apart from her two nights in a row to do his bills and play baseball, she becomes insecure and angry. Like a child who is upset when she can't see her mother, Iris becomes unnerved by the separation.

On the night her fiancé stays home to pay his bills, she calls to ask him how he is managing with his money. Later, she realizes that the real purpose of her call was to make sure he was still there for her. Her restlessness and anxiety cause her to pursue him in a way that is potentially stifling and alienating. She is unable to tolerate the frustration of his absence for two entire nights. She engulfs him emotionally in order not to be left again. If they have a fight, or even a small disagreement, she will buy him small presents to "show her love." Her "love" is really a desire to protect herself from loss. Her purpose is to ensure that he does not leave her—like her father did so often when she was a child.

Bud's struggle with intimacy is different from Iris's problem. He is the youngest of three children, and his mother and father divorced when he was seven. His father remarried when Bud was ten, and has seen him less and less often since then. Bud acts cynical and slightly suspicious about relationships. But at a party, he is the life of the crowd, full of wit and vigor. Yet it is hard for him to be serious and honest. He has male friends, but no one, he says, that he's willing to share his "dirt" with.

Bud may be reluctant to form deep relationships because he once experienced intimacy as a prelude to loss. At ten, his father was someone he looked up to, yet after the divorce his father drifted away. So now Bud works long hours, getting yearly raises and an occasional promotion, not simply because he's a good worker, but because immersing himself in his work protects him from the pain of being vulnerable again. Ask him out for dinner, and he says how much he would "love to see you," but he has "no time." He has no time for anyone.

Bud's father has moved away, but he still manages to teach his son. It's a lesson carved deep in Bud's heart.

"Everything I love goes away," Bud told me once through tears. "I'm sick of it. I just don't want to be hurt anymore. I'd rather be alone than be hurt. Being alone isn't so bad. At least you don't get chucked."

As deeply as Bud may be hurting, there's no need for him to stay in a condition of "aloneness." There is help and healing for the hurting orphan.

71

8

The Orphan's Need for Security

$\mathcal{M}$any of Charles Dickens's books have a character like Oliver Twist, a frail orphan who was born in a dingy poorhouse. Dickens's portrayal of the orphan is powerful because he experienced childhood isolation and orphan-like fears himself. He knew that without a loving, protecting father, the world can be a dark and scary place.

Because many novels have autobiographical elements, the character of Oliver Twist may offer insight into Dickens's own sense of isolation. Oliver was clearly born without a father, and from the first words of the story, the raw vulnerability and isolation of his life are poignantly clear.

> For a long time after it was ushered into this world of sorrow and trouble . . . it remained a matter of considerable doubt whether the child would survive to bear any name at all. . . . The fact is, that there was considerable difficulty in inducing Oliver to take upon himself the office of respiration—a troublesome practice, but one which custom has rendered necessary to our easy existence; and for some time he lay gasping on a little . . . mattress, rather unequally poised between this world and the next: the balance decidedly in favor of the latter. . . . There being nobody . . . Oliver and Nature fought out the point between them.[1]

According to Peter Ackroyd's extensive biography of Dickens, the book's plot was associated with "the pains of his childhood,"[2] including an incident in Dickens's childhood in which his father's unwise handling of money sent the man to prison for three months. Indeed, the entire family (with the lone exception of Charles) was sent to prison because of the father's indebtedness. For three months, Charles walked through a huge city alone, "cold, isolated, with barely enough to eat."[3]

Such experiences are not quickly or easily processed, and will make a lasting imprint on anyone—of any age. In the story of Oliver Twist, the newborn baby had to fight for the very air to breathe, a symbol of the orphan's struggle for life, for love, for everything. And, like the infant in Dickens's novel, the emotional orphan may not even be aware of his struggle—or its cause.

Pastor Fred grew up in a family with a very weak, passive father who was emotionally removed from the family. Because his dad was listless and disinterested, Fred never "connected" with him emotionally. Consequently, Fred has trouble "connecting" with and caring for the individual people he has been given to shepherd, and that's very bad news for those parishioners looking for his empathy.

When he was hired last year to serve in a moderately sized church, Pastor Fred surrounded himself with people who would support him. But it has become evident that he does not connect with them as people. They are impersonal pawns that he uses to prop up his empty inner world, a world in which he was left alone and undefended by his withdrawn father. When he talks about caring for his parishioners, he has no idea, really, what he is talking about; he is playing a role. He was never really cared for or valued himself, so he doesn't know how to care for the members of his congregation.

During Fred's therapy it seemed at first that I was simply a token therapist; he could be talking to anyone as long as he was getting attention. After two years, however, a slow change began to take place. Fred began to see me as a separate person; when I was out sick he seemed to genuinely feel for me, not just because he was missing what I could do for him in therapy. Slowly, but steadily, Fred has grown. In finding someone who genuinely cares for him, he has come to the place where he is beginning to be able to genuinely care for others.

Orphan psychology also affects how we respond to criticism. When we are put down and told we "are not quite right"—particularly by someone as important as a father—we can tend to see the entire world as a dark and unfriendly place, a place in which we feel outcast, rejected, and alone.

An emotional orphan who is criticized by a spouse, a friend, a lover, or an employer is likely to react with hostility or quick withdrawal. That's because the people closest to us shoot at closer range. And, if the father's critical nature has already left a scar, the orphan will be particularly sensitive to criticism.

Pleasing Others to Feel Safe

Tricia has always been close to her father. He is fairly intense, a real "go-getter" in corporate law. I would describe her as being very much like her father, because she has his high "standards," which she applies to her nursing career, relationships, morality, financial security, and her family. He taught her these things when she was growing up, through his own example and through regular, consistent criticism—most often the latter.

Tricia exhibits constant restlessness, though she does not appear to have a biological anxiety disorder. Her restlessness seems instead to be fueled by her desire to please so many people and, even more specifically, by her desire to avoid criticism, because "it hurts so much." She goes out of her way to please people in order to prevent their hurtful criticism or disapproval. During one session, when she was slouched down in her chair, looking totally out of it, I told her, "You look more tired and sleepy all the time."

She sighed. "Well . . . it's been a busy week, and I'm tired."

"What made it so busy?"

"I offered to stay late at work Monday because my nurse supervisor—she's a friend of mine—needed me to work a double shift. And Tuesday was rough because my friend from church had a baby, and I was organizing meals for ten days and cleaning her house."

"How did you come to do that?" I asked.

"Oh, I volunteered to do it at my local home group meeting. We usually do this for new mothers, and when no was else was speaking up . . . ah . . . the home group leader looked over at me and . . ."

"And you thought she wanted you to volunteer?"

"That's right. And then last night my mom asked me to help her set up the house for my cousin's baby shower. So I went over, and it took twice as long as expected. I guess it was fun—well, my mother seemed to enjoy it—but I never said I could stay for five hours."

"So why did you?"

"Because my mother would tell me she really needed me . . . or she would say I wasn't being thoughtful to my cousin if I left."

Tricia finds it painful to refuse anything to anyone. The more someone expects, the more she is willing to submit and ingratiate herself to them. She fears that refusing her time to someone will earn her criticism and, in a small way, rejection. She uses offensive pleasing to keep everyone liking her, and to prevent the pain of anyone criticizing her.

Using Criticism to Feel Safe

Tricia tries to please people to be safe, but Christopher manifests his orphanhood in defensive criticism. In other words, he believes in lowering the boom on the other guy before the other guy lowers the boom on him.

When Christopher was a child, his father was usually at work from eight in the morning until seven at night, and then was irritable when he got home. Generally, the family's priority was not intimacy; it was getting out of Dad's way and avoiding his verbal attacks. Christopher grinned when he talked about his home environment, but as the memories unfolded it was clear that there was nothing funny about it.

He became sad as he recalled being told over and over again to "be quiet." He said he rarely did fun things with his father. In one session, Christopher mentioned that his conception had been an "accident." He wasn't sure how he had learned this, but insisted that he had heard it a number of times.

He thought he had found the love of his life in Melanie, a girl he had dated for five years, but shortly after they became engaged she called it off.

I met him when Kate, his new fiancée, talked him into coming for premarital counseling. She felt that Christopher was constantly "adjusting her." As later became apparent, he had been quite hurt by his father's critical tongue, and his joking bravado was really a defense mechanism. When his ex-fiancée, Melanie, broke off their relationship, she added to Christopher's sense of disapproval. He never talked about his fears or insecurities, but dragged his feet in his relationship with Kate instead.

Most importantly, he was regularly critical of Kate. After discussing "the facts" over two sessions, Christopher began to listen to Kate's appeals that "he is trying to make me perfect before he will marry me." He initially thought she was exaggerating, but he slowly gained insight into his fear of a commitment to her, realizing that he was afraid to "take in" another person who could hurt him.

Orphans and Control

Margaret was molested by her father when she was about eight years old. She later learned that her younger sister had also been abused. She has had some counseling over the years and currently works in a department store. She has a couple of long-term friends, one of whom is her roommate.

Margaret came to see me because she was depressed and because she was having trouble with her roommate, who felt that Margaret's standards for cleaning the house were "to the moon." I assumed that meant too high, but Margaret liked things organized and clean. She also liked things clearly scheduled and predictable. If I kept her waiting for five minutes, she would become intensely annoyed; a cancelled appointment could ruin her entire day.

We eventually addressed her need for a controlled and ordered environment. When she was a little girl, her father's incest had subjected her to boundary violations that shook her deeply. In response, she tried to order her world in a way that compensated for the tremendous chaos of her home. Control, order, and predictability became her solution to her father's abuse. Unfortunately, she was still trying to offset her father's conduct in new environments and relationships that held no threat for her.

Margaret's need for control and order also translated into an acute concern for morality. She adhered to strict moral principles—and expected others to do the same—but she was motivated largely by fear, not piety. To her, morality was a way to control the world in the hope of preventing the kind of violation and trauma she had faced as a child. Because she had been overwhelmed by her environment in the past, she now wished that all those around her would act in ways that were morally predictable and safe. In this way Margaret is like so many with orphan emotions who try so hard to write a different ending to their experience, only to cause other problems with their "solution."

Orphans and Fantasy

Many father-child relationships are characterized by fantasy, especially ones in which a father is dead, absent, or abusive. If a father dies while his children are young, they may fill in the blanks, continuing their relationship with a fantasy father. Others use fantasy when their dads are frequently away from home, perhaps imagining their fathers working in faraway places. Still others use fantasy when a father inflicts hurts on them that are too distressing to face. Some in this latter group use fantasy to construct a romanticized view of their fathers, magnifying their fathers' good aspects and minimizing their faults.

The Orphan's Need for Certainty

Ron is a minister from Maryland. He sends me an occasional client as a "last resort." Before he referred the first client in my direction he wanted to meet with me a couple of times to make sure I was competent. Our lunches were nice breaks in the day; he has a delightful sense of humor. Nevertheless, I was struck by his sense of certainty regarding controversial issues.

Ron has a deep commitment to the Bible, and yet I believe his certainty has little to do with "faith." In fact, I think it is an example of his lack of faith. He was born in suburban Atlanta, the oldest boy in a family of five. He told me:

It would be two in the morning and my mother would be walking by my room to go to the hospital. She'd tell me that everything was fine, and that she'd be back in a few hours. But the redness in her eyes let me know that she was not fine. She'd tell me my father was ill and would probably be in the hospital for a few weeks. I didn't let it bother me. It had happened before and I could see the slight warning changes in his behavior. He would start talking faster and work more around the house. Mom would ask him if he was taking his medication. He would complain that he didn't like the way it made him feel, and after a while he would become irritable, and then he would start spending money. After that, he'd just disappear for a few days. Sooner or later, someone would see that he was acting bizarre and call the police. He'd wind up at the emergency room in the hospital once again.

Obviously, Ron did not have much stability in his home while he was a child. He could never be sure when his father would stop taking his medication and become manic or psychotic.

It may have been that uncertainty in his childhood that made him long for certainty as an adult. While I never did get to know Ron well, I was struck by his adamant feelings on difficult political, theological, and moral questions. He seemed to have all the answers, no matter how complex the question. Ron's opinionated views may have grown, to a great extent, out of the fathering he had received when he was a child. The point is that he brought his need for certainty, his fear of further chaos, to his reading of the Bible. And in the end he had more answers than Moses.

Now that we have discussed Margaret's need for control and Ron's orphan-like hunger for certainty, let's combine them. And I want to do it by talking about my father.

My father was not only intelligent, he was also driven. Once, looking back on his life, he told me, "Sometimes when I think about how I was back then, I sort of shudder. I realize now how much I gave to get out of poverty, as if I'd have been willing to sell my soul just to become a doctor and have a little money."

He was the tenth of eleven children, born in 1932, the same year his father walked home from his engraving work in tears because his pay had been cut in half. My father was too young at the time to understand it, but the story of his father's tears was retold on many occasions and was a source of fear to the entire family.

My father grew up in Lancaster, Pennsylvania, far from the Amish farms associated with the area. His family lived in a narrow, poorly heated row house with minimal insulation and a tin roof, and my father slept in the attic. In the winter he could see his breath, white fog floating out from under the covers to join with the fog of his three siblings in the same room.

My father was also deeply affected by wartime life. From the age of nine until the age of thirteen, he was faced with rationing. He would stand in line for meat, flour, and sugar. He vividly recalls regularly going to the meat market and waiting an hour in line for a pound or two of ground beef. And often after an hour wait there was no meat left.

During the war, he also came to realize that the poorer people were sent to the combat lines and exposed to the worst threats of the battle. Many of his older brothers-in-law were in the infantry or paratroopers. He also had a sister who served. But most disheartening was the death of his cousin, a man who lived only three doors up the street. Three others from his block also gave their lives in battle, and my father wondered whether the streets in affluent neighborhoods had so many dead.

My father especially wondered about this when he delivered newspapers in the Grandview area of Lancaster and saw the single homes with large, beautiful lawns. *Imagine actually having so much room that you wouldn't hear your neighbors' conversations through the wall,* he thought. *And you could play music and no one would complain about the noise.*

All these experiences combined to create a fantasy of a different life. A life with no wage cuts, cold winters, meat lines, or war dead. A world in which the privacy of a home was guaranteed, and one in which you were self-employed—and therefore in control of your own future. It was this fantasy that empowered him to spend thousands of hours in study to reach it.

Sometimes orphans become isolated by spending countless hours on their business or studies—whatever it is that will save them financially.

While my father had loving parents, he nevertheless had a specific area of orphan-like vulnerability. He swore that he would never be poor, no matter what it took. This is typical of the orphan mentality. Those who have experienced the economic vulnerability of the orphan often swear that they will never face it again. Some will do anything to avoid poverty.

The Orphan and Friendship

I first heard about the street children of Rio de Janeiro from my close friend Tim Manatt, a man who travels throughout South America and Mexico every year. He saw thousands of children living there in the streets. Such children have a great deal to teach us about the relational alternatives people use when they are alienated from their fathers.

Street children show us the importance of friends to orphans, or those with incomplete father relationships. They show us that friends can sometimes become a surrogate family, and any change in friendships can be very disconcerting for the orphan.

It is estimated that there are presently forty million abandoned children on the streets of Latin America's cities.[4] Some are "cute" children who can be seen begging at an airport or hotel, shining shoes, singing for small change, or carrying groceries; others are pathetic waifs, dope addicts, and irresponsible rebels.

While there are significant dangers from living on the street, one study showed that the physical and emotional health of the street children is often better than that of their brothers and sisters who remain at home.

> The street children have developed a level of life that very adequately compensates for the deprivations in their homes. The authors who have studied this phenomena note a significant difference in the average weight which favors the street children when comparing them with their siblings at home, which [is due] to better nutrition.[5]

Much of the research shows that these children, though mostly uneducated and illiterate, are surprisingly intelligent, and have a keen ability to take care of themselves. Indeed, begging in such a competitive environment is hard work that requires intelligence, social insight, and stamina.[6]

But some ask, "If these children are so smart, how do they come to live on the dangerous streets?" The answer lies in where these children come from. Most are not abandoned, but come from fatherless families. If a father or stepfather is present, he often makes the children work and hand over their earnings. With either an absent father or one who seems to care only about the money, the children begin to look to the streets for caring, secure relationships, often finding better relationships there than at home.[7]

In the streets, they find two key replacements: peer friendships and older, father-like males. The boys typically begin to investigate the relational options on the streets and discover that they are better than the options at home. At night these small boys can be seen huddled together under blankets or newspapers, squeezed into cardboard cartons, in ways that are a picture of the emotional comfort they find in these intensely close relationships. In the daytime much of their attempts at finding food or money are done together, and they typically share in each other's success.[8]

All of this makes me think of the dozens of adolescents I have treated, so many of whom have followed a path similar to that of these street children. These children began to look outside their homes for emotional replacements for their fathers (and occasionally their mothers). Their friends became their families, and their older friends or mentors became their heroes. While part of this process is typical of adolescence, it often occurs early or is more pronounced when the child feels like an orphan due to a mediocre father relationship.

Orphan Survival

While some of those with orphan feelings give up (emotionally or physically), many rise from their loneliness and make a decision to take care of themselves. They learn how to take the best advantage of any situation.

In the evening . . . [Roberto and Antonio went to fashionable Sixth Avenue]. After receiving some malignant looks and rude comments from people, they stopped on a side street where a rather young affluent couple were dining at an open-air restaurant, a few feet from the street. When the boys asked them for food, the couple tried to ignore them. The two boys sensed that they were intruding on a special occasion and so were insistent, thinking that they were likely to be paid to leave the diners alone. Finally the man who was dining told them in a loud voice to leave. When they did not, he called the waiter for help, who halfheartedly told the boys to go. They went across the street, maintaining minor eye contact with the diners, who were losing the pleasure of their occasion. As the waiter disappeared for the moment inside the restaurant, Roberto approached from one side and asked once again for something to eat; Antonio came from the other direction and grabbed a piece of meat off the man's plate. Running and laughing, they headed into the darkened street. . . . [And] tiredly entered their vacant corner, which they called "home."[9]

Could it be that Roberto and Antonio were not just trying to fill their empty stomachs? They might have met with quicker—and less risky—success elsewhere. The two boys seemed to be also working that day to fill their emotional hunger and emptiness, and their stimulating exploits helped them do that.

When you feel an emotional hole, you will look to anything that might possibly fill it. Sometimes individuals with orphan feelings use food, drinking, constant exercise, sex and aggression, movies, intense music, excess work, or drugs—anything to temper their sense of vulnerability.

Occasionally I see a desperate orphan-like survival reaction in the middle of marriage counseling. John and Lila had been married for six years and had one newborn child. After the baby's birth, Lila cut her work hours, bringing on new financial pressures, and John's work responsibilities were increased (with no raise). These developments added a significant amount of stress to their relationship. Both parents reacted like orphans.

"When I try to share my feelings he reacts and gets his 'Mr. Know-It-All' face on," Lila said. "I want to pop him one when he gets that pompous look."

"She can share all the feelings she wants," John chimes in. "It's not the feelings I get annoyed at, although the first three minutes in the door is hardly the time I want to hear them. Her expectation is that at any moment I will drop everything else and try to meet her needs."

"What is it you want from her, John?" I asked.

"You know . . . some space. A little bit of freedom. Not feeling as if I'm giving my last ounce of strength when I'm with her."

"And Lila, what do you want from John?"

"If I share my feelings with him, I don't want to be told that I'm wrong, and have him belittle me."

"Anything else?"

"Ummm . . . yeah. I just doubt that he's ever going to have time for me, because—"

"She says that even after I've been with her for three hours," John interrupted. "She *never* thinks I'm spending enough time with her, even when I've spent the entire weekend with her."

In listening to them, I was struck by their orphan-like insistence that they each be heard. They were unable to hear each other's concerns because they were in an "emotional protection mode."

John cried out for freedom and space because he could not find the emotional resources to listen to Lila's feelings. Lila thought that John should put her feelings above all else. However, John is emotionally impoverished; he has no "energy" to meet many of Lila's needs, and reacts by refuting her comments or intellectualizing them away. Basically, both of these people have decided that they will survive in this marriage—regardless of the cost to the other person. They will "survive" by talking over and over again about what each wants, by defending their individual rights—in short, by acting like orphans.

The Orphan's Loneliness

We can see, from John and Lila's example, that marriage does not prevent loneliness. In order to combat loneliness, a marriage needs a measure of intimacy and some wholeness from which to give. Loneliness can occur in the largest families, in the most crowded conditions, and at all stages of life.

One of my patients, a woman whose father was an irritable alcoholic, told me she used to fill her bed with big dolls and stuffed animals. Then she would cry herself to sleep at night as she heard her father ranting and raving throughout the house. Whenever he started shouting, she would clutch her big teddy bear in an attempt to find the comfort and protection she could not find in her father. She told me through tears that her best friend while she was growing up was that stuffed animal.

My ninety-year-old grandmother is far more mature than that little girl, but she fights orphan loneliness, too. She and I are very close and talk on the phone at least a couple of times a week. She still lives in her own home, alone, with an occasional visit from my parents. She explains how age isolates: "You reach your fifties and a few of your friends die. You are affected by it, but you have other friends and you move on with your life. But by the time you reach your eighties, your spouse has died, and any living friends have moved to Florida or are in a nursing home. Your body decays, and your knees hurt just to stand up. And going out looks more and more impossible because anything—heat, cold, whatever—really bothers you."

As my grandmother has aged she has increasingly talked about death, but I guess that is appropriate as her body grows weaker and her feelings of loneliness increase. Some say death is the one thing we do alone. It is the point of our greatest loneliness. But in the case of Mildred, I would have to disagree. . . .

The Loneliness of Facing Death

Some moments of aloneness are not everyday experiences. Life ebbs and flows, and so does the sense of isolation. There are valleys. And there are mountaintops.

My experience with Mildred was one of those peak experiences in isolation. She was the first person I ever escorted into death.

She was an elderly woman who had been hospitalized many times; she had been through radiation and chemotherapy for the lymphoma that had spread throughout her body. I was a raw, new subintern, a fourth year medical student, assigned to her for a month.

When I went in to see her for the first time it was 6 A.M. and she was sound asleep. I hated to wake her, but my job required it. Mildred was annoyed by the interruption. I apologized for troubling her, in a sleepy manner that only burned-out medical students can do, and asked if she minded my listening to her lungs. She said she was perfectly willing to do whatever I asked, just as long as I didn't ask her to use any of her own muscles. It was obvious that she felt miserable, but there was still a glimmer of her old mischievous nature showing through. She struck me as the kind of person who, as a child, had always gotten under her teacher's skin. I'm sure that she had been full of adventure and trouble, but wise enough not to get caught in her mischief. We became fast friends.

After a few weeks, it became clear that Mildred was going to die, but no one wanted to admit it. Her doctors procrastinated, but it was reaching the point where I felt she should be told where things stood. She would talk to me about what was going to happen when she went home, and I would sit there listening as if I thought it was really going to happen. It made me feel like a terrible fraud, so I finally asked the senior doctor's permission—which he granted—to talk to her about her situation.

Mildred accepted the news stoically. After we talked about her terminal condition, I came to see her two or three times every day. Her two daughters came to visit, too, but they had their own responsibilities and were already letting go—years of hospitals had worn them out. Soon our conversations turned to questions of faith. It seemed to be a comfortable place for us to be—a young doctor and a dying old woman, one person standing at the door of death, experiencing the ultimate orphan emotions, and the other acting as a simple human presence in the dark hospital room.

We prayed every day. Mildred said it helped for me to hold her hand and pray that God would be with her. She was so different from me. We were separated in age by half a century, of different gender, from different ethnic groups. I had nothing but a future, she had nothing but a past. But when we prayed, God changed the desperation of a dying orphan into gentle confidence and peace.

I was not with Mildred when she died. I had said good-bye the evening before and we had talked very seriously about her death. During our last conversation I told her I would see her on the other side, and I hoped she would be there to greet me when my time came to undertake the journey she was about to make. She smiled and nodded. She died early the next morning—sometime around 6 A.M.

The Orphan's Need for Security

Her death took me back to my first day with her, when I haltingly entered her room about that same time in the morning. I thought about isolation and vulnerability, and how, in the end, we are all orphans left to go on our final journey alone. I had walked her to the foot of the mountain and waved good-bye, but in the end she climbed alone. Yet I do believe that Someone escorted her on her final climb.

9

Orphans and Spirituality

*B*arbara was thirty when she first came to see me for depression.

"I want to tell you right off that I'm totally turned off to the idea of God right now," she began. "I've been so messed up by churches that I really can't handle any more of it."

"We'll talk about whatever you want to talk about," I reassured her.

"I just think back on all the weirdness I've seen in churches, and it makes me never want to go back."

She told me about attending parochial school when she was a girl.

"I got into Sister Ann's class, and she decided to give me a hard time. She'd throw erasers and yell and just terrorize us. I just decided that it wasn't for me after that."

But that hadn't been the end of her search. In college, a roommate had begun talking to her about God.

"What she said made a lot of sense, so I went with her to a few meetings at her church. After a while, I even joined. But the pastor was teaching some things I had trouble understanding, and I made the mistake of making an appointment to discuss them with him. He felt that I was against him just because I was asking some honest questions; he implied that if I didn't see things the way he did . . . well, then, I was full of pride."

After that experience, Barbara went to another church and eventually became very involved. She gave a tenth of her income, served the children's ministry, attended every service, and helped set up for and clean up after church functions. The church was a big part of her life until her husband left her for another woman.

"From then on it was like I was a leper. People at church would treat me as if I had a big 'D' on my chest for 'divorced.' They would avoid me. My best friends called a few times and then vanished. My bills started to stack up, and I asked the elders of the church if they could help me out."

She went on. "It wasn't as if I wanted a handout. I had worked hard for years, but I couldn't afford the mortgage and the legal fees on my salary. You know what they said? They said they wanted to investigate the circumstances surrounding the divorce. What does that mean? They had known me for more than five years. When did I become someone peculiar to them? There was nothing wrong with me when I had no major trials and when I was serving and giving them my money!"

Barbara was hurting, not only from the breakup of her marriage, but also from the treatment she received from some in her church. Though the elders eventually decided to give her $150, she felt the money had been given only to make the elders feel good about themselves rather than to provide any meaningful assistance; she returned the money and left the church, feeling abandoned and ostracized.

It's easy to understand why Barbara was upset.

Barbara, like many hurting people, hoped the church would refresh and strengthen her. She had only a fair connection with her parents, so she was hoping the church would fill in the gaps and be a caring comforter for her. But she, like many others, left feeling devalued and rejected. Such encounters with the church will make orphan feelings even worse.

Moreover, many psychological orphans find the concept of God very intimidating.

Larson is the father of three children, one of whom has Down's Syndrome, and he is intimidated by God.

"I've come to the conclusion that I am entirely expendable to God," he told me. "He can beat me, prune me, burn me out, do whatever he wants, just for the advancement of his name. I don't know . . . it's even hard for me to pray anymore, because the closer I get to him, the more pain I feel. . . . and the more seems to go wrong in my life."

Larson, whose father had been quite strict with him when he was a boy, had come to view God as a stern, overbearing father—one who regards principles more important than people.

In talking to Larson, it soon became apparent to me that he would often pray orphan-like prayers. He told me about an intense business meeting, and mentioned in passing that he had asked God to be with him. Later, in another session, he again mentioned that he asked God to be with him.

"Larson, when I hear you ask God to be with you, I wonder if you're really saying 'God is not with me.'"

"I don't understand what you're saying."

"Let me say it another way. When you say 'God, please be with me,' what is implied in that statement is that God is not with you at that moment. Right?"

"Well . . . I don't know about that. Are you saying that it's bad to pray?"

"Not at all. It's just that I think your prayers reveal that you feel lost and alone—maybe deserted by God. Each time you ask God to be with you, it may be merely a reinforcement that he is *not* with you—strengthening the core orphan sense that you live alone."

Larson didn't think my observation was relevant. Yet during our next session he told me that when he began thanking God for always being with him instead of begging God to help him in his times of trouble, his attitude improved.

Once Larson saw that the content of his prayers affected his mood, he began to look at his praying in greater detail. He came to see that despite all his talk about prayer, he really prayed for no more than a few minutes a day. He also saw that he had come to the point where his prayers were designed more than anything else to "appease God . . . to keep him off my back."

He felt that if his verbal offering was not put on the altar every once in a while, God might explode and hurt him further. He was not really seeking communion with God, but rather offering up talisman-type prayers to keep a harsh, punitive Father out of his life.

How to Discern Orphan Prayers

There are many different types of "orphan prayers," and it is not my intention to try to list all of them here. But I want to look at five types of prayer. The first three are prayers that may get in the way of an individual's relationship to God. The last two are prayers that can enhance the orphan's relationship with God.

1. Clichés or repetitious prayers

Jesus told us not to fill our prayers with "vain repetitions," as if God will hear us simply because of the repetition. A child who offers up a prayer such as "Now I lay me down to sleep" or "God is great, God is good" is doing well. He is just learning about God, and he can pray such prayers with the largest amount of feeling he can muster. But an adult who is still praying or reading rote prayers may not be praying at all. He may be just repeating words that don't really mean anything to him. He might as well be reciting the pledge of allegiance or a nursery rhyme. Otherwise, he would be using words, concepts, and emotions that an adult would use in a conversation with another adult. Prayer is not the recitation of a magic formula; it is an intimate conversation between the creature and the Creator.

An orphan may want to hide behind clichés and prayer formulas because he is afraid of God.

I'm not talking about the originality of the words you use when you pray, but about your sense of closeness to God as you pray them.

2. Praying about others

"Wait a minute," someone may say. "I thought that praying for others was an act of selflessness. How can that be bad?"

It can be a way for the person who's praying to avoid going to God about his own feelings and his own needs. It is good to pray for others, of course, *unless* it is done as a means to keep the spotlight off your own ambivalent relationship with God. Praying about others can be another way for the orphan to hide from God.

3. Sharing personal thoughts with God

This is when prayer is made only at the thought level, with no regular emotional vocabulary. If we think about human relationships, it is certainly true that it is generally easier to tell someone your opinion about a movie you've seen or a book you've read than to tell the person that you are angry, jealous, or insecure. I think this is also true with God. It is important to go "deeper" than this, and pray more specifically about the way you feel—to discuss your feelings and motives on a more intimate level.

4. Sharing general emotions with God

In this type of praying, one shares feelings directly with God, using a feeling vocabulary that contains words such as "afraid," "insecure," "hurt," "angry," "jealous," and "suspicious." For example, "Lord, I felt angry today when my boss corrected me in front of the staff. It made me feel like a fool." Or, "Father, I get insecure and angry with you when my car breaks down two months in a row. It's not like I'm a rich person with money to throw around." It is okay to be completely open and honest with God. He knows your feelings already, and it will only deepen your relationship to share them openly with him—to put into words what is already hidden in your heart.

5. Peak prayer

In this closeness with God, one is praying one's deepest heart and experiencing a special sense of being God's child. For some, this includes a sense of being heard and understood by God, or a sense of having the Spirit of God "bear witness" to their spirit. For others, it may be the experience of having a Scripture verse suddenly seem to jump off a page, or a sermon hitting them straight on in response to a prayer.

Some of these peak experiences are subtle and may just involve the gentle, comforting sense that one is not alone in the universe. Others involve more dramatic connections, such as the experience of an old friend of mine, Brother Harry.

I knew Harry when he was nearing the end of his life, residing in a nursing home. I always liked to visit him, and had a good time talking with him about everything from coal mining to faith. I have rarely met a man who loved the Lord more than Harry did.

On one occasion he told me about an experience that had happened when he was in his fifties. He said that he had been praying upstairs in his room, as he did every night after dinner, when he felt certain that God was directing him to go visit a man named Ed Quinlanson (Harry didn't know anyone by that name).

Harry grabbed his coat and headed out the front door, confident that God would direct him to his appointed destination.

"Where in the world are you going?" his wife called after him. "It's freezing out there!"

Sure enough, it was cold . . . and snowing, too. But Harry could not shake the feeling that he *had* to find this man named Ed Quinlanson.

As he stepped out onto the street, a friend came driving past in a pickup truck. The man slowed down and called out, "Harry . . . are you crazy? What are you doing out in this weather?"

"I'm on my way to meet with Ed Quinlanson," he answered.

"Then let me take you," the friend offered through his window. "I go right past his house."

Harry was happy to accept the ride, and even happier that his friend recognized the name. When they reached the right road, his friend pointed out Quinlanson's house and sped away down the street. Harry walked to the door, shivering as the cold wind tore through his coat.

Mr. Quinlanson's daughter answered his knock, and then went to get her father. A man about Harry's age came to the door and asked what Harry wanted. What could he say? It's not as if he had training in this kind of strange experience. But he figured that if God had told him to come, then it probably had something to do with spiritual matters.

"I'm here because I believe I'm supposed to talk to you about the condition of your soul," Harry said matter-of-factly.

After the door was slammed in his face, Harry stood outside for twenty minutes in freezing temperatures. Finally the daughter let him in, and prevailed upon her father to give him a few minutes.

Harry asked the man one question about his past experiences with God, and Mr. Quinlanson talked for an hour about the betrayals and hypocrisy he had experienced in churches in the past. Apparently, decades earlier, his faith had been precious to him, but he had been disillusioned and had not set foot inside a church for over twenty years. Harry empathized with Ed's disillusionment but said that when Ed turned away from God he had lost his best friend. He asked permission to pray for Ed.

Ed joined Harry in prayer, the first he had prayed in years. After it was over, the men smiled broadly at each other through tears. Soon afterward, Harry left.

Harry later learned that Ed Quinlanson had died the very next day.

A relationship with God is the most pivotal relationship a human being can experience, and I believe many people who think they are tasting it are only smelling the stew.

Part of the reason some people have trouble entering into a relationship with God and staying with it is because of their difficult relationships with their earthly fathers. I have even met theologians whose residual father experiences left them alienated from God. In the next chapter, we'll look at why some people are bored with or disinterested in God, and we'll also consider the psychological profiles of some of history's most famous atheists to see if we can discover the source of their alienation and distance from God.

Part **3**

······································

The Fatherhood of God

10

Why Can't I Love God Like I Want To?

Some people have no interest in God and do not care about their spiritual side. Others consider themselves believers but rarely feel close to God. Does this reflect your experience? Do you feel close to him once in a while, but consistent closeness eludes you? Are you feeling alienated from God but can't quite figure out why?

There are many possible answers for this alienation.

Someone says, "You are obviously involved in sin of some kind and that has separated you from God."

Someone else offers, "Brother, when you've been a Christian as long as I have, you'll realize that those emotional rushes are only for new believers. That dullness you're feeling is natural . . . so don't worry about it!"

Another observes, "I've noticed you've been sad for a couple months now. Maybe you have a chemical imbalance of some sort."

All these notions may have elements of truth. The dullness people experience toward God may have many causes, including unethical acts, wrong expectations about the Christian experience, even biological imbalance. And yet there is another serious reason that is very hard to detect. It is a tendency to see our own fathers' defects mirrored in our relationship with God.

Ana-Maria Rizzuto writes about Sigmund Freud, the father of modern psychology. "Throughout his long life," she writes, "Freud was preoccupied with the question of religion and more specifically with the psychological origins of God. He made a strong case for a direct correlation between the individuals' relation to the father . . . and the elaboration of the idea of God."[1]

Freud's writings repeatedly questioned God's existence. When someone as brilliant and innovative as Freud calls belief in a Father God foolish, it will have a marked impact. The intellectuals who heard him thought he was using cold reason as the basis of his atheism; it is possible, however, that his atheism had very little to do with reason. His atheistic beliefs may have been attacks on the father he despised.

One modern student of Freud, the psychologist Paul Vitz, has shown case after case of famous, outspoken atheists who have had what he calls "a defective father"—that is, a father who is abusive, weak, absent, or even deceased.

According to Vitz, Freud was not only estranged from his father, Jacob, but was in many ways his father's antithesis. Jacob was an observant Jew who read from the Hebrew Bible and Talmud daily, who would not defend his Judaism or himself. If a man knocked his hat off and called him a "dirty Jew," Jacob would not bother to respond. Sigmund, in contrast, was not only willing to brawl when faced with anti-Semitism; he was also quick to engage in many fierce intellectual battles throughout his life.[2]

Sigmund perceived other weaknesses in his father. The elder Freud was unable to provide financially for his large family, so they often had to rely on the generosity of others. Moreover, as an adult, Freud alluded to his father as a "sexual pervert" in letters, and considered the possibility that Jacob was not really his father.[3]

Freud is not the only major thinker with a defective father relationship who became a skeptic; Vitz lists many other examples:

- **Voltaire**—The famous anti-Christian philosopher so strongly rejected his father that he discarded his father's name (it is believed that "Voltaire" may be a reconstruction of his mother's maiden name). His first publicly performed play was called *Oedipus*, which had reference to the Greek story in which a son kills his father. He entertained the idea of being someone else's son and was ashamed of his father's middle-class heritage.

- **Ludwig Feuerbach**—A famous German "anti-theist" philosopher of the nineteenth century, who considered religion merely a "dream," lost his father at the age of thirteen when the man abandoned his mother and began living with another woman in a nearby town. The scandal and rejection felt by a child in conservative nineteenth century Germany were no doubt enormous.[4]
- **Karl Marx**—This influential originator of modern communism despised his father for rejecting a rabbinical tradition that ran through both sides of the family by converting to Christianity for social reasons. Marx proposed that the destruction of religion was a necessary prelude to global happiness.
- **Friedrich Nietzsche**—The well-known father of the "God is dead" philosophy was insistent about the need for man to function alone. He stressed that human beings are orphans and not God's children. His father died when he was four years old.[5]
- **Bertrand Russell**—The Nobel Prize winner who was considered one of the finest and wittiest thinkers of the century, wrote two books discussing the foolishness of religion. His father died when he was four.[6]
- **Jean Paul Sartre**—The French novelist, dramatist, and philosopher, who argued militantly against God's existence, lost his father before he was born.[7]
- **Albert Camus**—The French novelist who wrote *The Rebel*, argued for rebellion against a number of things, including God. In *The Stranger*, he portrayed a condemned man facing death serenely in an impersonal cosmos. His father died when he was one year old.[8]
- **Madalyn Murray O'Hair**—One of America's most influential atheists, a woman who has been instrumental in removing much of traditional Judeo-Christian values from public schools, once tried to kill her father with a butcher knife. She did not succeed in killing him, but screamed, "I'll see you dead! I'll get you yet! I'll walk on your grave."[9]

Not all atheists believe as they do because of defective father relationships, but many of the most influential atheists in history have been tragically estranged from their fathers. Few—if any—ever recognized or acknowledged the role their fathers played in the development of their theories and personal psychologies, but their relationships with their fathers were nonetheless influential. We *all* have fathers living in our hearts in ways we do not see, and they often acutely affect—for better or worse—our relationships with God.

The next chapter discusses the way the Creator has revealed himself as a Father, and how he has pursued people like you and me to be his children. We will discuss his revelation of himself as an adopting Father, a Father to those who consider themselves orphaned or fatherless, and a God who has used the fatherless as his key ambassadors to humanity.

Bible Fathers from Adam to Jacob

*Y*ears ago, when I was in medical school, I often turned to the beach as a place of refuge and safety.

The work demands were far beyond what was reasonable, and sometimes I was completely overwhelmed. The hours I spent sitting on the beach, looking out to the horizon, brought me a great sense of peace and comfort. The rest helped, of course, but it was more than inactivity that refreshed me.

The ocean seemed to go on forever. The sky also seemed limitless. These two infinities, two forces extending into the distance, helped to lift me out of my sense of vulnerability, my profound awareness of my own limitations. That setting helped me focus more on God. And it made me realize that I was not in intimate connection with God anymore. I had let my busy schedule crowd him out of my life.

There on the beach I knew that God was with me. I was restoring my relationship with him; I knew that I was safe and that I was not alone.

Much of life is really an attempt to feel safe and emotionally connected in this way, to get to the place where we feel joined to Someone who understands our struggles, Someone who cherishes and protects us.

Perhaps the innocent crayon artwork of children shows this best. Children's pictures often contain images of the orphan. A little girl draws a picture of herself in a boat out on a lake, all alone. A little boy's picture shows him standing alone in a field. Why do children so often portray themselves as alone? Perhaps it is due to a threatening environment—these children's drawings often depict a father figure with a scary face or some other menace—a stepfather, an uncle, a dangerous neighborhood, or an abusive school environment.

Do you feel the need for a safe place, a need for connection? If so, listen to the Scriptures, because they paint an awesome image of God's desire to fully and intensely meet the orphan's emotional hunger.

Creation and the Rescue of the Orphan World

Scripture opens its pages with the powerful assertion, "In the beginning God created the heavens and the earth." Bruce Waltke, the renowned Hebrew scholar, explains that this bold assertion is a summary statement of the creation. The actual record of creation begins with the next line: "Now the earth was formless and empty, darkness was over the surface of the deep, and the Spirit of God was hovering over the waters."[1]

The image at the start of creation is that of a dark world, desolate and unappealing. The creation account portrays an unsafe place, clothed with chaotic waters, dim and forbidding. But that was before God stepped into the picture—before his power and love created the first humans and brought order and unity out of chaos.

God is still very much involved in the creation business today, and on one dramatic occasion I had a front row seat.

I remember running to the delivery room to assist with the birth of a child. It was about three in the morning, and at that time of day my thinking resembled the primordial chaos mentioned above. Unless one is a veteran to the Labor and Delivery Ward, there is nothing casual about the birth process. Thankfully, as a medical student all that was expected of me was delivering straightforward cases with supervision close by.

This was a straightforward delivery. It was the woman's fourth child; she was familiar with labor, and the baby came forward normally. As the baby's head crowned, I applied appropriate pressure to prevent any tearing of the woman's skin. The head came out in a controlled and gentle manner without incident.

Good, I thought, as I checked the baby's neck. *No umbilical cord.*

Next, I grabbed the suction bulb and suctioned clean the baby's mouth and nose. Then I rotated the baby's head downward. Pressing the head downward slightly allowed the upper shoulder to slip out. Then, as I gently pulled the head upward, the lower shoulder slipped out. Finally, I crouched with the baby in my hand, trying to gingerly allow the rest of its body to slide out.

To my relief, the baby slipped out nicely; a unique being now breathed—for the first time—in my arms. Though I had delivered infants before, I was struck once again by the marvel of this new creation.

In the midst of my moment of wonder, the baby's mother leaned forward and asked the sex of the child.

"It's a boy," I told her.

The mother immediately let loose with a string of profanity that would have reddened the ears of a sailor. "I wanted a girl!"

I tried to understand the woman's feelings, but I was nonetheless saddened that this child should be so rejected on the day of his birth. Would every birthday be like that first one? Would that child always be an emotional orphan?

Contrast that event with the image of Adam's entrance into the world. The great Renaissance artist, Michelangelo, depicted the creation of the first man in a fresco that adorns the ceiling of the Sistine Chapel in the Vatican. The painting depicts the creation of Adam as an event that is at once both momentous and intimate. The contrast between the child I delivered and the creation of Adam is striking. God as Father is not merely present, but is the primary creative force for bringing Adam to life.

But the biblical depiction of Adam's entrance into the world exceeds Michelangelo's portrayal; God is more than a casual Creator pumping into Adam a vague, impersonal, creative energy. The Bible says that God breathed "the breath of life" into the man, an act that (according to Derek Kidner) is "warmly personal, with the face-to-face intimacy of a kiss."[2]

God is not merely a watchmaker, piecing Adam together like a combination of tiny gears and springs; he is Adam's Father. Later in the Scriptures, Luke writes a genealogy of early man that includes Adam and his descendants, saying that Seth was the son of Adam, and Adam was "the son of God" (Luke 3:37). We are also told in Genesis that Adam and Eve were made in the image of God, and Adam's children were conceived and born "in the likeness of Adam," further demonstrating the Father-child relationship God wants us to have with him.

The character of that Father-child image is shown in the dependency of Adam and Eve as recorded in the Genesis account. It is striking how the newly created adult humans are as needy as little children. They appear disoriented and unsure of themselves. Yet the Father is prepared to address this, and places them in a special place to live, a place created to please and marvel them. At the same time, he gives them responsibility and freedom.

Imagine God reaching into a universe of helter-skelter darkness and shaping it into a comfortable and hospitable home for the humans he was about to create, then reaching out to the soil of the earth to create those humans. Dirt is not an appealing thing, yet it was this form of matter that God chose, instead of diamonds or gold, as the substance that he would tenderly and lovingly mold to create the first man. Those first chapters of Scripture portray a divine parent moving toward a human child, anticipating and providing for the needs of that child instead of avoiding or ignoring him.

And even after early mankind rejected God's Fatherhood, God still sought to reconnect with them. God still wants to give his children a safe place to live, and a way to be reconnected to him. Therefore, he has provided a way for salvation and adoption, so that human beings can safely "come home" to him. He acted to adopt humans back in earlier times, and he continues to adopt humans now.

How does God communicate his plan for adoption and for a new world? Interestingly, God typically appears to use people with orphan-like experiences or those who are in a fatherless state as his ambassadors to humanity. Perhaps this is because these fatherless allowed God to fill their emptiness with his presence.

Therefore we see that God's fatherhood has a number of major dimensions. His attempts at help are broad; his care addresses our need for never-ending intimacy, our need for a safe place to live, and our longing for a Defender when the world seems to be against us. We can see that demonstrated in the lives of several of the great heroes of the Bible, beginning with Noah.

How Noah Faced His Greatest Challenge

Noah was the son of a man named Lamech, and both had an intimate relationship with God. Lamech sensed that God had a special purpose for his sons. And Noah, a man who "walked with God," clearly had a purpose.

One day God came to Noah and explained that the earth was no longer safe for his descendants because it was filled with "extreme violence," and that he was planning to send a catastrophic flood. Apparently, it was a rare time in history where humanity was becoming perfectly evil and there was no hope of reaching them. God commanded Noah to build a massive watercraft that would be used to save him and his family during the time of God's judgment on the earth. Noah's father, Lamech, died about five years before the flood; Noah had to face that worldwide cataclysm without the help of his beloved father.

Imagine the isolation Noah must have felt, living as he did in such a violent generation, knowing that all those around him were going to be destroyed. Noah's intimacy with God—and his eccentric mission—had very likely cost him any friends he might have enjoyed, but that loss was probably nothing compared to the emptiness of completing his watercraft without his father's companionship. After he had grieved for his father, Noah then had to leave behind all the places that he had known as "home." As he and his family entered the craft, the rains began to fall, and "home" became nothing more than a memory.

As the craft moved on in the dark waters, how uncertain Noah must have felt. He had no father to give him advice, no one to turn to but God himself.

Here again we see the themes of God's adoption of his children. Noah floats in the chaos of the dark, rainy waters, which are reminiscent of the universal chaos that existed before the creation of man. He is fatherless, defenseless, and vulnerable, with no clear understanding of what the future will bring.

And yet, perhaps it is Noah's vulnerability and his need for God that make him so useful. It is during the chaos and the lonely darkness that he is partaking in the salvation of mankind. He is functioning as the Father's agent, taking his family into a new life. Noah's journey of faith resembles those of so many other ambassadors of God in which their vocation is empowered by the loss of their father. Noah steps out into the watery, black chaos as an orphan, and there God proves himself a Father to the fatherless. In the exact symmetric center of the story, the part of the account an ancient reader would have regarded as primary, we read the words, "God remembered Noah."[3]

What striking words! How meaningful to know that when you are on a dangerous voyage into the unknown, an eternal Father "remembers" you and has you on his mind. Noah lost his entire culture and faced the greatest cataclysm in history—yet in the midst of this emotional turmoil he was not an orphan; he was not forgotten; he was carried in an intimate and protective fatherly manner through the disaster so that he could serve as an ambassador to a new age of man. The story of Noah shows us that when we are fatherless, God fills that void with his fatherly love.

He did the same thing in the life of a man named Abraham.

An Orphan on a Journey of Faith

Abraham grew up in Ur and was the child of Terah, a man described as an idolater. We know little about the relationship of Abraham and Terah.

It was not until Abraham was seventy-five years old that his father died. At such an advanced age most people are not thinking about taking up a new vocation. But it was at that point that Abraham, newly fatherless, began his mission. Once his father died, Abraham's relationship with God appears to have intensified. He buried his father, packed his belongings, and led his wife and servants on a journey into the unknown, headed for a place he had never seen, to find a vague "promised land."

Once Abraham had begun his journey into uncharted territory, into places full of mystery and violence, God came and made a special covenant with him. His first recorded words to Abraham were, "Do not be afraid. I am your shield, your very great reward."

Indeed, God blessed Abraham so much that he became known as "the father to the faithful," and ended up acting as God's ambassador to the entire world. So large is the influence of this man—an influence that began after his father died—that God said his descendants would outnumber the stars in the sky and he would be the father of many nations.

After making that promise, however, God directed Abraham to take his only son, Isaac, to a sacrificial mountain and offer him up as a sacrifice—much as the pagan cultures of the day often did with their children. Abraham didn't understand how he would be able to become the father of many nations if his only son were killed, and he must have questioned why God would ask him to do something that seemed so contrary to God's care. But he obeyed, nevertheless, and traveled up a mountain, prepared to offer Isaac as a burnt offering.

Imagine how Abraham must have felt as he climbed that mountain, preparing to sacrifice his son. He ascended the mountain with no support except God. Having buried his father at Haran, he went up the mountain to meet his toughest test, to face his worst fear—losing his son.

Yet Abraham obeyed. At the moment when Abraham chose God's will over his son's affection, God intervened. Abraham's choice took him to another level with God. He had become a man who would obey God no matter what. At the same time, God proved that he was *not* the type of sadistic god worshiped by the surrounding cultures; he said dramatically and emphatically, "I do not want human sacrifices. I will never ask you to sacrifice one of your children to me. I am your loving Father." And, in that event, God foreshadowed the day when a loving Father would give the ultimate sacrifice—his only Son, Jesus Christ—for the sins of the world.

A Con Man Named Jacob

What we are seeing in our journey through the Scriptures is that God is a Father who is faithful to the fatherless, who does not abandon us, even when we don't deserve his presence.

The twenty-seventh chapter of Genesis tells the story of Isaac's son, Jacob, who donned a disguise in order to dupe his elderly father into giving him the blessing that rightfully belonged to Jacob's brother, Esau.

Jacob obviously yearned for his father's endorsement, because he was willing to break his father's trust and risk his own life to receive the blessing that should have gone to Esau. Having stolen the eldest son's blessing (a very serious offense in ancient times), he had to flee from his brother in order to save his life. As he fled, he traveled alone. How often have we seen this picture: a figure facing isolation and an uncertain future, alone and orphan-like? He may have wondered whether he would ever see his aged father again.

Jacob rode into an unknown future with the guilt of his unscrupulous actions, and the knowledge that his deceit had been exposed. He had betrayed his father's trust and became a fatherless refugee.

But God, Jacob's heavenly Father, immediately came to him in a dream. Jacob saw a stairway resting on the earth and extending into heaven. Above the stairway God spoke.

> I am the Lord. . . . I will give you and your descendants the land on which you are lying. Your descendants will be like the dust of the earth. . . . All peoples on earth will be blessed through you and your offspring. I am with you and will watch over you wherever you go, and will bring you back to this land. I will not leave you until I have done what I have promised you.
>
> Genesis 28:13–15

That account reveals God as a Father who is eager to meet the needs of the fatherless as soon as they appear. How different God's fatherly care is compared to some earthly fathers. One of my patients, a woman named Lily, illustrates the contrast.

Lily, a fifty-two-year-old mother of two, was the first in her family of five children to attend college. Her father owned a retail store on the edge of a moderate-sized Southern town. She says that when she went off to school in Chicago, she had the sense of "going it alone," with no father reaching out to comfort her.

"How were you alone during college?" I asked.

"It started as soon as I was leaving. My father gave me a few dollars, kissed me good-bye, and then sat down to continue reading the paper."

"What were you hoping for?"

"I wanted him to watch me drive off. To look sadder. To have him say he would be thinking of me. This is stupid for me to say. I feel silly saying it. All this was so long ago. The man's been dead for more than ten years."

"What was it like to leave home?"

"Well, I acted braver than I really felt. It was a very long drive—took me days. And when I got there I called home to let them know I was all right."

"And maybe to reconnect a little," I prodded.

"Yes," she replied. "My apartment was small and I was living alone. No one was there to greet me or to help me move in. It was hard those first weeks."

"So what happened when you called home?"

"Well, my dad answered the phone, and just about the first thing he said to me was that he was surprised I was calling long distance. He didn't even seem to be relieved that I'd made it okay . . . like he hadn't been worrying about me at all. As I hung up, he told me to drop them a post-card."

"And that bothered you?"

"It was like he was saying, 'next time, write, don't call.' I felt that I had screwed up by wasting money calling them. I regretted doing it."

Lily's and Jacob's experiences are quite different. They are different because God is a different kind of Father. He reaches out to the father-less; he carries the orphan lovingly through the struggles of life.

Yet the emotional orphan is likely to wonder, "When push comes to shove, Father, are you really going to be there? Are you really going to take care of me? Do you really love me?"

Such questions are at the heart of orphan fears, fueled by past vul-nerabilities that left pain. Orphan fears are so important that the Scrip-tures do not avoid them but give many accounts of lives full of orphan feelings and experiences.

12

Bible Fathers from Joseph to Moses

*J*oseph was a special child. He was clearly his father's favorite, and his brothers hated him for it. They resented his grandiose dreams and his relationship with their father.

Joseph once had a dream that his brothers would bow down to him, and he wasted no time before he told his brothers all about it. They became so enraged at their seventeen-year-old brother that they wanted to kill him. However, one brother was able to prevent the killing, and Joseph was sold into slavery instead.

Like so many heroes of the Bible, Joseph's adventure started when he was separated from his father and entered a life with God as his Father and guide.

Joseph was sold to an Egyptian official, and was very successful at running the man's home. Unfortunately, he was eventually accused, unjustly, of trying to seduce the captain's wife, and was thrown into prison. Yet even there Joseph's faith in God was evident.

Eventually, Joseph's intimacy with God resulted in his ability to understand dreams. Thus, when Pharaoh, the ruler of all Egypt, had a confusing and troubling dream, Joseph was summoned to interpret it.

Not only did Joseph correctly interpret the dream, but Pharaoh was so struck by the "spirit of God" in Joseph and the strength of his presence that he made him the second most powerful man in the entire nation.

The dream warned of a famine that was coming in seven years. When it came, thanks to Joseph's leadership, Egypt was ready, with a surplus of grain. Thus it was that Jacob and his dubious children, the same ones who had earlier sold their brother into slavery, found themselves going to Egypt to buy grain. In the end, they all survived only because Joseph had been sent by God to go ahead of them. What his brothers had done decades earlier with violent hearts, God used to save not only his family, but an entire nation.

And despite all that Joseph had been through, despite the intensity of his intimacy with God, Joseph still longed for his earthly father, and still desired his father's respect and love. After receiving his brothers and offering them his forgiveness, he urged them to bring his father quickly, a message that echoes the common desire of all humans to be received and respected by their fathers.

When his father arrived in Goshen, Joseph took his chariot out to meet him. When Joseph saw him, he "threw his arms around his father and wept for a long time" (Gen. 46:29). Joseph had a great hunger for his father, and in Joseph's case, God reunited the two men after twenty-two years of separation.

Moses—The Fatherless Liberator

After hundreds of years had passed, a new dynasty came to power in Egypt that saw the growing numbers of Hebrew people as a threat to its power. Consequently, the rulers of this dynasty turned the Hebrews into slaves. Not only that, but an order went forth that all newborn Hebrew boys were to be killed.

Thus, when Moses was born to Jochebed and Amram, Jochebed hid him for three months. But then, realizing she could no longer keep him hidden, she prepared a basket to float the child in the plant cover along the river's edge, while his sister watched over him. A daughter of Pharaoh heard the child crying when she went to the river to bathe. She took the child as her own, and even wound up hiring Jochebed as a wet nurse to care for him.

For the first four or five years of his life, Moses lived with his mother, who nursed him, and with his father, who taught him all about God.

This time obviously made a deep and lasting impression on Moses, because later in his life he identified with the Israelites.[1] Yet, after those few years with his father, he was removed from his "caretakers," adopted as the legal child of Pharaoh's daughter, and raised in the distant home of his enemies—the rulers who had earlier tried to harm him.

Moses lived in the luxury and splendor of the palace until he was forty years old, but he never forgot who he was or where he came from. Then one day, when he saw an Egyptian mercilessly beating an Israelite, he killed the Egyptian and buried him in the sand. When his crime was discovered, he fled for his life to the land of Midian.

Isolated from his family, a refugee in a strange land, Moses tended sheep for forty years. There he developed a relationship with a priest named Jethro and married the man's daughter. When Moses was eighty years old, God spoke to him in a miraculous way from a burning bush and told him to return to Egypt as the deliverer of the Hebrews.

Moses' experience again reveals how God chooses many of his leaders from the fatherless. Moreover, the Exodus account might well be viewed as the record of God's dealings with an entire nation of orphans, a people who were defenseless and vulnerable, who were living as degraded slaves. But some may ask, "If God loved his nation of orphans so much, why did he let them be slaves?" Perhaps because the Hebrew people before Joseph had become horribly corrupt and violent by their constant association with Canaanite peoples. According to professor Bruce Waltke, the only way God could keep his people safely isolated from Canaanite barbarisms such as child sacrifices, religious prostitution, and sorcery was by putting them in Egypt. You see, Egyptians hated shepherds and so the Jews were left uncorrupted in the bosom of Egypt.

When a new dynasty arose that enslaved and threatened his people, God acted on their behalf once again.

The certainty and inevitability of God's purpose was evident in Moses' role. God did not send Moses with a diplomatic proposal; he told Pharaoh what *would* take place. God is not weak, no matter what most of us believe about him at times. Religious people commonly say that God is strong, but they often show by their actions that they really think he's powerless. Those who have had a weak or passive father may be more likely to entertain such ideas about God, because they find it hard to believe in a strong father—earthly *or* heavenly. But Moses did trust in God's strength.

As he walked before the grandeur and power of Egypt's throne, it must have been hard for Pharaoh to take him seriously. After all, the Hebrews were an "orphan" people. They were the refuse of the Egyptian culture, abused and degraded; their lives meant nothing. They had no land, no power, and no status.

But what the powerful pharaoh couldn't see was that God was this "orphan's" Father, and thus the power that created the universe was represented in this old, stammering man named Moses.

God showed the Egyptians that he "meant business" about the deliverance of his people by bringing a series of plagues on the nation. First, he turned water into blood. Then, at Moses' command, he sent plagues of frogs, lice, flies, boils, cattle disease, hail, locusts, and darkness.

But Pharaoh was not moved. He was not inclined to let his slave labor leave Egypt. So God himself came to Egypt to save his children from captivity. We need to understand and appreciate the serious nature of that visit; God's act of war on behalf of the orphan nation Israel was like dragging the sun into the center of the country.

Before God could come to save his children, however, he needed to prepare them. Because his power and purity are inseparable, his children had to conform to his nature before they could profit from his power. So he told Moses to celebrate the Passover, in which a lamb's blood was placed on the doorposts to protect the Israelites from the powerful, moral Presence of God. The conditions of their deliverance illustrated that God is not only a Father, but that he is also pure in a way that is beyond our comprehension.

Through the Passover, God showed his supreme power *and* his complete acceptance of his children. That night when the Presence of God came, there was no inquiry at the door. God did not ask the people inside if they were "good Jews" or "bad Jews." The blood on the doorposts showed their faith and their obedience, and all who were covered by the blood were spared God's fury.

But God also showed mercy on Egypt. He did not destroy the entire nation in blind anger, as he could have. Egypt had been destroying and killing God's firstborn, his children; so the Egyptians, including Pharaoh, lost their firstborn children as well. Only when that loss touched Pharaoh, when he saw the totality of God's power, did he finally agree to release the Israelites.

As you read about the release of the Jews, does it seem unreal? Do you struggle to see God's power in your life? Do you feel as if your father has been a weak and emotionally defeated man most of his life? Does the idea of leaning on a father—earthly or heavenly—seem like someone else's experience rather than yours?

Diane felt that way. Her father worked as a pharmacist; her mother ran the household. Diane explained that her mother ran things in the manner of a drill sergeant.

"Where was your father in all this?" I asked her.

"He just faded into the woodwork," she answered. "He let my mother tell him what to do about everything. Whenever he was home, he was more than happy to let Mom run the show."

"He was pleased by the way your mother ran things?"

"I wouldn't say he was pleased. I mean, I don't ever remember my father being *pleased* about anything. In fact, he always seemed defeated at breakfast—before the day had really even begun."

"And what was your response to this?"

"I'm sure I resented it . . . and I found myself protecting him from things that I thought might upset him. For example, when I lost a job at the paper company, I didn't even tell him until I had found a new one, a month later, because I wanted to protect him. I guess I was acting as his parent—sort of a role reversal."

She went on to say that her father was easily frustrated and threatened by small comments and changes.

"If, on a Saturday, I asked him if I could do a chore later on in the day so I could spend some time with a friend, he would get very upset. If I tried to change anything it was like I was personally attacking him; he would come unglued."

Diane's experience may be more typical in some nationalities and ethnic groups than in others; the myths of some cultures include father-gods who are weak and powerless. The father myths of such cultures probably reflect real experiences with this type of father. John Miller, in his survey of Near Eastern myths, notes that the father deities in these stories are often marginal, incompetent, and powerless.

How different is the Father God of the Israelites. He does not need to be protected, like Diane's father. Instead, he comes and enters the pain to heal it. He doesn't need to be babied, because he has limitless resources. And he has the strength to be a defender to his child, whether that child is an entire nation or an individual man or woman.

Joshua—Bringing an End to Father Abuse

When Moses died, the leadership of the Israelite nation was passed to a man named Joshua. Roughly two million people looked to this man for guidance. Imagine the challenges he faced. Not only did he have to assume leadership of the Hebrew nation, but he had to do so while on the way to war.

Why were they on their way to war? How could a loving God allow such a thing? I believe part of the answer has to do with the terrible mistreatment of Canaanite children that was taking place at the time, and God's desire to defend the fatherless.

The land the Israelites were going to fight for had been promised to Abraham hundreds of years earlier. At that time, God had told Abraham that the land would be given to his descendants, but not right away. Why not? Because, as God said, "the sin of the Amorites has not yet reached its full measure" (Gen. 15:16). God would not take the land away from its current residents without a very good reason.

But apparently things had become so bad by Joshua's day that God felt the time had come to remove the people from the land. The children of Israel were instructed:

> When you enter the land the LORD your God is giving you, do not learn to imitate the detestable ways of the nations there. Let no one be found among you who sacrifices his son or daughter in the fire, who practices divination or sorcery . . . [or] engages in witchcraft. . . . Anyone who does these things is detestable to the LORD.
>
> Deuteronomy 18:9–12

Over the last decade I have met and worked with a number of sociopaths, men who have committed terrible acts and felt no guilt about them. Yet I doubt that any of them would do what is described above—behavior typical of the nations inhabiting Canaan in Joshua's day. Can you imagine the sort of culture that would allow a father to sacrifice his children in a fiery offering? I find it horrifying just to think about, and it was obviously horrifying to God as well, because he felt their violent occult religion was beyond redemption.

In recent years, archaeologists have discovered some ancient prayers of the Canaanites to their gods. A typical prayer is, "A firstborn, Baal, we shall sacrifice, a child we shall fulfill." Jewish history includes the account of a battle in which King Mesha of Moab took his own son, the crown prince, and publicly offered him as a sacrifice. The Israelites were so horrified by this act that they completely retreated.[2]

God says repeatedly throughout the Bible that he is a "Father to the fatherless" and warns with straightforward firmness that those who threaten or victimize the fatherless will find a lion waiting to defend them. One biblical passage offers the sober warning:

> Do not . . . encroach on the fields of the fatherless, for their Defender is strong; he will take up their case against you.
>
> Proverbs 23:10–11

The destruction of the Canaanites represents a unique event in history. It was a judgment against a specific people who terrorized and abused their children in abominable ways. The severity of God's reaction to that abuse shows how far God will go to protect the fatherless. This is not to say that God will destroy every person who abuses the fatherless; he is merciful and patient. Even the Canaanites were given ample time to change their ways before judgment fell on them. But make no mistake—God will defend the fatherless by any means possible—including, if necessary, the destruction of their abusers.

But God's concern for the fatherless extends beyond preventing or healing the effects of abuse; he is not only a Father who protects, but also a Father who believes in and supports his children.

13

David—The Adopted Son of God

• •

*I*magine what the prophet Samuel was thinking when he came to the town where David's family lived, looking for the next king of Israel. Perhaps he was reflecting on the last man who had been anointed king of Israel. Saul had turned out to be an impossible man, an unworthy king, and an abusive father. At one point he even threw a spear at his son (and you thought your dad was moody!).

Samuel had been entrusted with a number of key roles in Israel. As a child he had probably rarely seen his own parents while being raised in the distant temple. But God had nurtured him and ultimately made him a national leader, a judge, a prophet, and a priest. God had spoken to Samuel when he was a child; now he was given the task of discerning and anointing the kings God had chosen. As he entered David's hometown, he was probably not only reflecting on how disappointing the last choice had been, but hoping that the new king would do better.

God had told Samuel that the new king would come from among the sons of a man named Jesse, so Samuel invited the entire family to a special meeting. Jesse didn't bother to invite his youngest son, David, to the meeting; he apparently figured that the young man was too small and too insignificant. He couldn't see the potential God saw in the boy.

You see, when he was growing up, David had spent a lot of time by himself, out in the privacy of the grazing lands, and during those times he had developed a real love relationship with God. It was David's "heart for God" that caused him to be given the gift of kingship—though he was the youngest in his family. So, upon being summoned late to the meeting with Samuel, David was anointed the future king of Israel as his surprised family looked on.

David didn't take the throne immediately; he was to succeed to the throne upon Saul's death. Yet even after he was anointed by Samuel himself, David still didn't get much respect from his family. His older brothers had gone to fight in Saul's army against the Philistines, but David was too young to go. After a while, Jesse sent his youngest son to the Israelite camp to see how the older boys were doing.

David's brothers weren't all that happy to see him. His oldest brother verbally degraded him, saying, "Why have you come down here? And with whom did you leave those few sheep in the desert? I know how conceited you are and how wicked your heart is; you came down only to watch the battle."

"Now what have I done?" David asked. "Can't I even speak?"

Even as they argued, David and his brothers faced another confrontation. A giant Philistine by the name of Goliath came out to taunt Saul's army. Every day, Goliath would come out and challenge the Israelite soldiers, offering to fight the bravest and strongest man among them. If he were victorious, the Israelite army would surrender; if the Israelite soldier defeated him, the Philistines would surrender.

There were no takers. This Goliath was one huge, fierce-looking guy, and all the Israelites were afraid. The only one who wasn't afraid was little David. He was indignant.

How dare this Goliath taunt God's people this way? David reasoned. And how could the Israelites be so fearful, when God was on their side?

It was up to David to fight Goliath, and that's what he did—despite his brothers' objections and ridicule. You see, David knew that his Father was with him, and that meant that he would prevail. So David placed a smooth stone in his sling, let it fly, and destroyed the fierce Goliath with a single shot.

When you are facing the threats and challenges of life, knowing that your father believes in you is very important. And David shows us that it doesn't have to be your earthly father who believes in you and gives you this support. It can be your heavenly Father.

David's life was not free from problems and mistakes. He made many errors in judgment that caused him grief and undermined his household for generations. But still, because he had a close relationship with his Father God, he became the most powerful and influential king in Israel's history.

When Rejecting a Father Leads to Greatness

Have you ever heard the expression, "He comes from a long line of drunks"? Or, "Their family has always been that way"? Or, "She's just like her father"?

Most often, people say such things when a child misbehaves. Yet Scripture shows us examples of children who rejected their fathers' examples and stopped the cycle of tragedy.

Josiah was the seventeenth king of Judah, a man who came from a long line of troubled fathers. His grandfather Manasseh is remembered as one of the worst kings in Jewish history, and his father, Amon, wasn't much better.

Josiah became king at the age of sixteen. Perhaps because he had no earthly father to lean on, he reached out to God. As the years passed, Josiah was able to return the nation of Israel to its original purpose—exemplifying a people chosen to be the children of God. Josiah removed the pagan altars that had been set up throughout the land, stopped temple prostitution, made great strides toward ending paganism, and used his own money to facilitate the worship of God. He still stands in Jewish history as a child king who "turned to the LORD . . . with all his heart . . . soul and . . . strength" (2 Kings 23:25).

Another example of someone who broke with her father is a woman named Ruth. Ruth's famous words (which she spoke, strangely enough, to her mother-in-law) are often quoted at weddings: "Where you go I will go, and where you stay I will stay. Your people will be my people and your God my God. Where you die I will die, and there I will be buried."

Ruth was a Moabitess who married the son of Naomi. Over time, both Naomi and Ruth lost their husbands, and their futures looked doubtful. Naomi insisted that Ruth would have a better future if she returned to "her people and her gods." But Ruth decided to turn her back on the gods of the Moabites, perhaps because they were so different from her thoughtful and kind nature. For example, Chemosh, who was the chief god of the Moabites, was worshiped through the sacrifice of small children.

For whatever reason, Ruth refused to follow the familiar beliefs of her pagan fathers. Instead, she decided to follow the truth. Such an act of independence is not for cowards. It can be extremely difficult for adult children to follow a faith different than what they grew up with, because they know their families will be disappointed.

But Ruth had come to love the one God of Israel, and she would not turn away from him. And if you turn to the short Old Testament book that bears her name, you'll find out how well that worked—for Ruth *and* Naomi.

Ruth's act of separating from her father and following a different path is one we all do to some degree—we are not to be clones of anyone. And yet in some families the process of growing up and becoming a separate, unique person is thwarted. Intimacy with God often helps this process because developing a Father-child relationship with God makes you less dependent on your earthly father.

Do the Fatherless Rule the World?

Perhaps after taking a look at some major figures from the Bible, you're getting the impression that God keeps people in cold storage until they become fatherless. That is overstating the point I want to make, but it is true that many heroes of the Bible began their richest experiences only after God filled their fatherless void with himself.

But perhaps you are thinking that this only applies to biblical figures—that those were special situations that are irrelevant to your life in the here and now. It may be easier to believe that God could look after Josiah than it is to think he will take care of you. But Paul Tournier, the famous Swiss psychiatrist, in his book, *Creative Suffering*, points to the fact that several of the world's most influential leaders have been fatherless or orphaned in some way. He describes how one of his colleagues,

Dr. Pierre Rentchnick of Geneva, studied biographies of the world's most influential politicians. Tournier writes:

> He was soon struck by the astonishing discovery that all of them had been orphans! Some had lost their fathers in infancy or in early youth, others their mothers, and some both parents, or else they had been cut off from one or the other because they were separated; or else they had been illegitimate children and had not known their fathers or anything about them. Yet others had been rejected or abandoned by their parents. Dr. Rentchnick compiled a list of them. It contained three hundred of the greatest names in history, from Alexander the Great and Julius Caesar, through Charles V, Cardinal Richelieu, Louis XIV, Robespierre, George Washington, Napoleon, Golda Meir, Hitler, Stalin, to Eva Peron, [and] Fidel Castro.[1]

I was fairly skeptical about this at first, but then I started looking at some of the most recent United States presidents. There was an obvious pattern.

Just before Bill Clinton was born, his father was killed in a traffic accident. Then, when young Bill was four years old, his mother married Roger Clinton, the man whose name he bears. His new stepfather was an alcoholic; he was abusive and highly unstable. When Clinton was fourteen, he was forced to stand up to this violent man in order to protect his mother and his little brother, Roger. Thus, he was thrust into the role of father and protector at an early age.

Ronald Reagan's father was an alcoholic, and when he was still a boy, Reagan found that he was often forced into the parental role.

Gerald R. Ford was originally christened Leslie L. King Jr., but after his parents divorced and his mother remarried, he took his stepfather's name. Ford went without seeing his "real" father for years, and described him as "a carefree, well-to-do man who didn't really give a damn about the hopes and dreams of his first-born son."[2]

Dr. Rentchnick suggests that father deprivation produces "a will to political power."[3] Being an orphan, whether in a literal or figurative sense, can produce an extraordinary, consuming motivation.

This drive is not limited to politics; it also influences religion. Rentchnick is quick to point out that "the Buddha, too, was an orphan, as was Mohammed, whose father and mother both died before he was one year old!"[4] To that list, we can add Gandhi, Ignatius Loyola, Martin Luther, John Calvin, and Confucius, who were either rejected by their fathers or lost them in childhood or early adolescence.[5]

In other words, in politics and religion, the child who is faced with abandonment or rejection often turns the rejection into a drive to transform the world. And, as we can see from the names that were listed by Tournier, this drive is not always beneficent. Orphans have been among the best and worst of human leaders. Some are driven by their orphanhood to reach for the stars in anger and enmity, while others reach the heights of love and service to God and humanity. Many waver between the two extremes.

The drive for power—if not attended by God's blessing—can create more problems for the child who has been deeply hurt. The "easiest" response for some fatherless individuals is to let the drive for power consume them, but that may ultimately destroy them and their loved ones. It is crucial for the urgent drive created by emotional orphanhood to be tamed—by intimacy with God. He can heal the wound that fuels the drive and promote satisfying creativity, which is not driven by fear.

Not only do the fatherless often attain great political power; they also frequently display great creativity. Paul Tournier was orphaned at the age of five—and he has written some twenty books. Glancing through the biographies of modern actresses, actors, and popular musicians will reveal many who have endured father deprivation or orphan experiences. Dr. Andre Haynal, famous European psychiatrist, feels it is not the will to power that is the strongest force in these people, but their creativity. His list of creative artists and writers who endured some form of orphanhood includes Leonardo da Vinci, who was an illegitimate child, and Johann Sebastian Bach, who was an orphan, as well as Rudyard Kipling, Leopold Tolstoy, Dante Alighieri, and Fyodor Dostoyevsky.[6]

It is apparent that God often blesses the fatherless with extraordinary power, vision, and wisdom. You see, God is often the strongest in us and through us when we are at our weakest and most vulnerable point. But he does not merely give us strength from far off. God's greatest sign of intimacy is to fully enter our weakness. His supreme humility is the act for which he is treasured throughout the world.

14

The Day the Father Came to Earth

• •

I am writing this a month before Christmas. As I look out my window, I can see a few homes already decorated with lights. One has
tiny, white, twinkling lights. Another has the older, large red and green
bulbs. Some have candles in the windows. My house, on the other hand,
doesn't even have a cardboard paste-up picture of Santa.

But it wasn't always this way.

One year, early in the season, I decided to get a manger scene for the
front yard. So I went to the local superstore to look for one.

"I'm looking for a manger," I told the young man behind the counter.
"A Christmas manger."

"No problem," the young man said enthusiastically. "I'll take care of
it right now."

What a joy it was to see this fine young man, so anxious to please,
even in the crush of holiday shoppers.

I was daydreaming about how fine the manger would look in front of
my house when my reverie was interrupted.

"Here he is," the young man announced; I looked into the smiling
face of his colleague.

"Here who is?"

"You know," he said. "He's the one. I got him for you."

I still didn't understand. "Got who?"

"The manager," he said. "You told me you wanted a manager."

That young clerk had apparently never heard the word "manger" in his life, and so must have thought that I had one of the world's all-time strangest accents, somehow transforming "manager" into "manger." Finally, though, I was able to explain to the two men what I really wanted. They pointed in the direction of "Aisle six . . . the Santa aisle."

Aisle six was easy to find, but it wasn't really what I wanted. There were about two million Santa dolls, but not a single manger scene—not one sign of the real meaning of Christmas. Not one decoration to show appreciation for God the Father's most precious gift to mankind—his Son.

I guess I shouldn't have been surprised that Jesus was ignored at the local store, because history tells us that this is exactly the reception Jesus Christ received in Bethlehem when he was born. He was unwelcome; he had to be born in a stable. Yet Christ was the one who was referred to in prophecy as "the everlasting Father," or a "Father forever."[1] With this name he represents our supreme Mentor, the fatherly older brother so many longed for growing up. Jesus was also called Emmanuel, or "God with us." He was the power behind the creation of the universe, yet he came to us in weakness and humility.

When God came to earth in the weakness of a mere man, he revealed himself simultaneously as Father and child. Jesus' incarnation illustrated and underscored the fatherhood of God and modeled the kind of relationship that's possible between Father and child.

A Tale of the Father's Love

One of the stories that best shows the Father's love is Jesus' tale of the prodigal son. The story (from the Schaller Condensed Version) goes like this. A man had two sons. One day one of his sons asked for his half of the inheritance. After receiving his money, the young man left home for a far-off land, where he quickly blew the entire bundle on a wild life of parties and "fun." When his money was gone, his "friends" deserted him; he sank into a pitiful, demeaning routine. Alone and penniless, he felt an urgent desire to go back home. He knew that his father's servants had plenty of food to eat, so he decided to return home and ask if his father would accept him into the house as a servant.

But that's not what happened. As he was returning home, even while he was still "a long way off, his father saw him and was filled with compassion for him; he ran to his son, threw his arms around him and kissed him." And then his father hosted a huge feast to celebrate the young man's return.

But that's not the end of the story.

There was an older brother involved, an older brother who had never given his father a day of trouble in his entire life. He was a "good boy," and he was proud of it. When he returned from his hard work in the fields and learned of the celebration that was going on just because his loser of a brother had come back home, he was furious.

And he let his father know exactly how he felt.

"All these years I've been slaving for you and never disobeyed your orders. Yet you never gave me even a young goat so I could celebrate with my friends. But when this son of yours who has squandered your property with prostitutes comes home, you kill the fattened calf for him!"

The father responded to his "good son" by gently reminding him of their closeness. "You are always with me," he said, "and all that I have is yours." But the father went on to explain that it was right "to celebrate and be glad," because his brother "who was dead" had come back to life.

Even today, two thousand years after it was first told, this is a powerful story. But when we place it in the context of the culture in which it was first presented, it has implications for the fatherless that are spine tingling.

Kenneth Bailey, a man who has immersed himself in the traditional folk culture of the Near East,[2] explains that Near Eastern peasants had strong reactions to some of the story's situations. For example, when the prodigal asks for his share of the inheritance, he is actually saying he wants his father to die. Peasants from Algeria to Syria who heard the prodigal's story all expected the father to respond violently to his son's request, because they interpreted it that way. Any peasant youth who made such a request would surely have been beaten. Further, the prodigal's departure for another country communicated that he couldn't have cared less about providing a respectable burial for his father. His leaving represented a spurning of his family, his clan, and his village.[3]

The prodigal's behavior was not only a statement of outright rejection and hatred for his father; his riotous living would have brought shame and dishonor upon the father, even if those acts were done "far away."

It's interesting to note that the prodigal did not consider returning home until he had sunk so low as to desire to eat and sleep with pigs. Why did he wait so long? Perhaps part of the reason is supplied by Bailey's Near Eastern peasants. They explain what would normally happen if a son returned home under such circumstances.

First, his father would ignore him as he approached the home. The village gang would see him coming and would shame him in front of everyone. After this "welcome-wagon" experience from the village, he would arrive at the gate of the house, where he would sit, perhaps for many hours, while his father *thought* about letting him in. When he was finally permitted to enter the house, if permission came at all, he would be punished so that the father's honor would be preserved. In Jesus' story, the youth's fantasy is to return home and become a lowly servant in his father's house, which was probably a realistic expectation of what he could expect from a father he had betrayed and shamed in such a way.

But the father in this story does not allow the village gang to shame his son as he approaches. He does not exact revenge or administer judgment. Indeed, even though the father has been mistreated by his boy, he takes further humiliation on himself by running out to meet the young man. Such an act of running would have been considered profoundly embarrassing in Eastern culture, as Bailey explains:

> A man of his age and position *always* walks in a slow, dignified fashion. He has not run *anywhere* for any purpose for forty years. No villager over the age of thirty ever runs. . . . To [run], he must take the front edge of his robes in his hands like a teenager. When he does this, his undergarments show.[4]

When the father reaches his son on the outskirts of the village, he makes it easy for him to come home. He kisses him repeatedly, requiring that the servants respect him by placing one of his best robes on the young man. And he orders a feast complete with music and dancing, so that the village elders will either have to accept the son or risk alienating the father.

The core of much of this tale, however, relates more to the older brother than to the prodigal son. The brother had been doing the right thing—he had stayed home and looked after things, and was even out working hard while everyone else was celebrating. Bailey shows us that the good child is not really so good. At such a feast, the elder son would be expected, by custom, to converse with the seated guests while he stood and served them. He would offer them the choicest pieces of meat and say, "Eat this for my sake." He would be expected to shake hands with all the honored guests.

Yet this "good son" publicly insults his father by questioning the man's mercy. He refuses the feast and his rebuke to his father is immediately known to everyone. As Bailey says:

> Nothing is secret in the village. . . . The older son's rebellion . . . is just as serious as the earlier rebellion of the younger son. Everyone in the banquet hall tenses expectantly, awaiting the father's decision. They assume that the son will be punished immediately, or ignored until the guests are gone. Then he will be beaten properly.[5]

But the father again reacts in an unexpected way; he goes out to plead with the son to join them. He obviously has no intention of responding harshly to his son. But the elder son continues to shame his father, committing his offense in front of any observers, which probably included various levels of servants, lesser guests, unidentified bystanders, and the village boys milling around. The father, however, does not allow the embarrassment to cloud his affection for his son, and makes a gentle appeal to him, reminding him of all the love and commitment he has for the young man.

This story illustrates the Father heart of God, a Father who makes every effort to take our shame away from us, whether we are disheartened by our actions, feeling proud of our superiority, or wavering between both. And really, Jesus' story is more than a tale; it is an invitation to accept the acceptance God offers. Regardless of our shame or embarrassment, in spite of our past hurts or insecurities, our Father God is waiting. He will run to meet us, he will greet us magnanimously, generously. He will lavish affection on us. He will forgive our misbehavior and forget our mistakes. All we need to do is turn to him and accept our Father's love and generosity.

Jesus as a Model for Fatherless Children

Scripture teaches that Jesus was born of Mary, but that he was also the Son of God; his birth was not the result of a union between Mary and her husband, Joseph. Jesus seems to have understood, from his earliest years, that Joseph was not his "real father."

When Jesus was a boy, his parents would take a yearly Passover trip to the temple in Jerusalem. On the return from one such journey, Jesus became separated from his parents. Joseph and Mary traveled for a day before they realized he was missing from their band of travelers. Finally, after three whole days of searching, they found him back in Jerusalem, discussing the Scriptures with the teachers and amazing them with his knowledge.

When his parents found him they were naturally quite upset.

"Why have you treated us like this?" Mary asked. "Your father and I have been anxiously searching for you."

"Why were you searching for me?" Jesus responded. "Didn't you know I had to be in *my Father's* house?" Christ's words show that he did not see himself as Joseph's son. He would certainly have loved his "stepfather" and followed his direction, but his primary father bond was to God, even when he was a child.

It appears that Jesus experienced much earlier than most the sense of having surpassed a father in a certain area—which creates a fatherless feeling. When a child surpasses a father in skill or understanding, for example, he or she will probably feel alone, in new territory. Many men and women have described to me the friction they have had with their fathers when they either surpassed them or differentiated themselves in some way. For some this has involved embracing a new denomination or faith, pursuing a different career, reaching a higher level of relational maturity, or simply attaining greater knowledge. Jesus probably understood these feelings because he apparently surpassed his parents' spirituality as a boy.

We do not know when Joseph died. It may have been when Jesus was an adolescent or in his early twenties. But Jesus had been enhancing his relationship with his eternal Father from his earliest years. In fact, God's fatherhood was the core message of Christ's ministry. Jesus said he came to "manifest the name of God," and, according to Joachim Jeremias, Scripture records more than 170 instances of Jesus addressing God as Father. Jesus modeled for us how an individual should relate to God—as a child relating to a father worthy of trust.

A study of Jesus' life will show that our Lord often sought to spend intimate times alone with his "Abba" (Father). Three theologians from the ancient church, men who probably had Aramaic-speaking nurses when they were children, testify that "Abba" is how small children in Jesus' culture addressed their fathers. The Talmud says that newly weaned children learn to call parents "abba" and "imma."[6] Jesus demonstrated that child-like intimacy in his relationship with the Father, and in so doing taught the immense value of child-Father tenderness with God. He said that we must be like little children to enter the kingdom of heaven.

Rags to Riches for the Fatherless

One of the most important works of Jesus is his involvement in our adoption by God. What Jesus did for us reminds me of the movie classic *Oliver*, in which an orphaned little boy dreams of a stable family. The child's life is desperate; each day is a struggle for survival. His longing for love leads him into some unwise friendships, and his lack of fatherly guidance leads him to identify with any thief who will give him a moment of attention.

Oliver fights against extraordinary odds and suffers innumerable losses as the story develops. He seems to have little hope for a better life. And then, suddenly, his whole world is changed. He is found by a loving, adoptive father—one with strength, affection, and financial means.

What a delight it is when the kind Mr. Brownlow adopts Oliver as his own. We know that this honorable man will be a terrific father. Brownlow provides a happy ending to Oliver's story.

Jesus is the means whereby your life and mine can have a happy ending. Jesus saves us from isolation. He brings us into a Father-child relationship with the Creator of the universe. By accepting Jesus Christ we are spiritually united with him, and so the Father regards us in the same way he regards Christ—with love, acceptance, and even pride!

Sixteen years ago, Dr. Ian Jackson, a surgeon from Scotland, visited Peru to do some work among the poor there. Just before he was to leave, a two-year-old Indian boy was brought to him. The orphan had a hole in the center of his face. He had no teeth, no upper lip, no nose; all the bone that normally surrounds a nose was gone. He had two eyes and a jaw up in the middle of his forehead. Dr. Jackson said, "It was a very complicated problem and I obviously [could not] do it in Peru. . . . If he came to Britain, yes, sure, I would be prepared to do whatever I can."[7]

Much to Dr. Jackson's surprise, the Indian boy (who later became known as "Dave") arrived at Glasgow airport a few weeks later. Many onlookers in the airport were horrified at the mere sight of him, but Dr. Jackson and his family took Dave into their household. They adopted him as their own. For Dave, coming to the Jackson's home meant being fed physically and emotionally.

> He had never seen food like we had. He would eat scraps off of our plates. He ate the butter out of the dish simply because he was so malnourished.[8]

Perhaps the most startling aspect of Dave's story is what happened after he looked in a mirror. Dr. Jackson needed him to see why he was going to be operated on. He needed to know why the pain of the surgery was necessary.

When he saw the image and suddenly realized, *That's me,* he was devastated. It was an awful but inevitable experience, one that hurt both the surgeon and the little boy. But out of this anguish was born a shared participation in the re-creation of Dave's face. And so the little boy from Peru surrendered himself to "a series of surgeries in Glasgow, borrowing bone and skin from one part of his body or another to form a new face."

> And he—he just looked in amazement and he said, "Am I going to have a nose, a real nose like everyone else?" "Yes. Well, at least [we're] going to try and . . . give you a nose like everybody else's." "Oh, that's marvelous," he said. . . . And then the next thing he wanted to know was, would it be a big nose?[9]

Slowly, Dave's adopted father rebuilt his face. It took more than eighty operations, but he did get the new nose he wanted, "along with a new upper lip made from his tongue, a new palate and a new upper jaw." Today, eighteen-year-old Dave has very intense emotions about his father's work. Despite the pain of the process, he regards his father's work as "amazing" and "incredible." He entrusted himself to his father, and his trust and confidence grew every step along the way. Now he says, ". . . there's going to be another one where my dad's going to make it straight and then afterwards he might transplant some hair to make a mustache and then revise the total scars on my body and then make my lip thinner—you know, just detailed things that I—that I would like personally."[10]

Dave has lived a very unusual life. But are his emotional struggles entirely different from yours? Like so many of us, he had a biological father who could not help heal his crisis. When Dave looked in the mirror he hated what he saw and was overwhelmed with shame and worthlessness. He also struggled with an urgent sense of emptiness, hungrily gobbling butter from a dish and eating it plain.

Dave brings to mind the pain we have experienced in isolation, perhaps far away from a father's help. He is a concrete image of our feelings of not being quite right—emotionally or physically. He demonstrates that sometimes we yearn for a "food" that is, at times, barely definable.

In Dr. Ian Jackson, we see a portrait of the fatherhood of God. He is a tender Father who enters our pain and does not shrink from our dark side, a Father who loves us when we feel unworthy. Being adopted into a relationship with the Father surpasses all else in life. Indeed, much of the pursuit of money and fame and pleasure is really yearning for God. Let us find our joy in discovering our place as beloved, secure, cared-for children of almighty God. Perhaps you're asking yourself how this takes place. How does one concretely and specifically heal fatherless yearnings and grow into a secure child of God? There are steps you can take to actually heal father hunger and father hurts. These include investigating your father's world, determining what shaped his deficiencies, and dealing with the resentment you feel towards him. Later, we will discuss how to find a mentor to help meet the needs that your father can't meet, and I'll suggest ways to stay connected to the perfect father—God.

Part 4

Rebuilding Your Father Relationship

15

Putting Your Heart Back Together

*L*auren was a pleasant, intelligent young woman, but she was haunted by a ghost—the ghost of an unpleasant, frightening memory that had haunted her for more than fifteen years.

"I'll never forget being eight years old and sitting in the back seat with my little brother. My parents were fighting. They were always fighting. I always got upset when they fought, and I begged them to stop, but they just ignored me. My mother was driving when all of a sudden my dad got so mad that he just grabbed the steering wheel and turned the car right toward a tree on the other side of the road. At the last minute, he turned the wheel back and my mother and I started crying. I never really trusted him after that. I hated him." Her eyes filled with tears at the recollection of this incident from long ago.

"Is this why you're coming to see me?" I asked.

"Not exactly." She paused for a moment and went on.

"I've been dating Bob for a while now," she said. "We care about each other, but we fight a lot, too. It can get really ugly sometimes. . . ." Her voice broke off and tears spilled from her eyes and ran down her cheeks. It was a few minutes before she was able to continue.

"We were driving the other day, and he was really upsetting me. He hurt me so bad that I just had to stop him, and . . ."

"And what?" I asked.

"I grabbed the steering wheel and turned it toward a tree!"

She was horrified that she would do the same thing her father had done fifteen years earlier.

Lauren is not alone in her repetition of her father's behavior. Unresolved emotions toward our fathers are dangerous for many reasons, but particularly because our fathers' attitudes and behaviors are more easily reenacted by us if they have not been purposely confronted and resolved. As voiced in Harry Chapin's classic song, "Cat's in the Cradle," we commonly repeat many of our fathers' behaviors—especially those that hurt us. It is impossible to magically remove these troubles from our personalities. But God wants to rebuild the inner psyche in all of us. Part of that includes working through and processing the memories of our fathers, working through our "father issues."

Processing your personal father memories requires a number of things. Perhaps the most important of these is a commitment to reality. Decide to be honest—honest about your resentment and his failure. Quick, magical forgiveness is usually dishonest denial. You will need to slowly process the anger, guilt, or fear you feel concerning him. You will need to learn how to handle traumatic father memories. You must find out how to get unstuck if you have been unable to grieve. And, finally, you must discover how to come to peace with your father—whether he is dead or alive.

Do You Really Know Your Father?

Part of the "reality principle" mentioned above is seeing your father in his cultural frame. If your father hurt you or ignored you as you were growing up, you may find it very hard to be curious about his world. It is easier to ignore him or withdraw from him. An angry patient once said to me, "Why should I care about his life? He rarely cared about mine."

But for the sake of your own mental health, you shouldn't do that. Why not? Because your father is in you. His likeness dwells in your body, his words echo in your mind, his fears move you, and his dreams motivate you. There may be pain in your father-child relationship, but such pain must be confronted and metabolized. Stuffing it down inside will not work. It will still be there, crouching inside you like a jack-in-the-box, waiting to leap out the minute someone opens the door. The anger or hurt could come out at others or cause you to do unhealthy things as you attempt to heal yourself. You could be like Lauren—surprised to find yourself doing what you hate. Therefore, in order to deal with the pain you feel, it is imperative that you understand your father as well as you possibly can. Wouldn't it be nice if the domino effect stopped with you, and a new healthier legacy were started?

What Was Your Father's Cultural and Family Language?

I'm writing this book in English. It's easier for me to write in English because that is what I have been hearing for decades. I have been exposed to German, Greek, Hebrew, and even a dash of French as a toddler, but English is my language. If my survival depended on navigating through restaurants using any of those other languages, I would certainly starve to death within a week.

Family assumptions are much like languages. We learn, largely by the example that our parents set for us, that certain behaviors are right or wrong. We learn to "speak the language" of the family. "This is the way we have always done things in this family" becomes a standard to live by.

There are also certain cultural traditions and expectations that permeate any society. For example, American culture plays a significant role in our relationships with our fathers by defining how children and fathers should behave.

1. Emotion training of men in American culture

If you grew up watching movies featuring Clint Eastwood, Charles Bronson, and John Wayne, you may be inclined to believe that American men should not display any emotion—except, perhaps, anger or aggression. Conventional male wisdom says that displaying one's emotions is a feminine trait, and males simply cannot run the risk of being called a sissy.

Our culture has long communicated that if a boy or young man is not "tough enough," he is a failure as a man. This thinking still flourishes. I was visiting a church service not long ago in which the minister talked about training his son. Apparently the seven-year-old had fallen and skinned his knee. He came running, crying, into the garage where his pastor father was working with a friend, rebuilding a classic car. The minister shared with his congregation that he told his son to "suck it in and act like a man," because he did not want everyone treating the boy like a wimp. While his intentions may have been good (protecting the boy from those who might pick on him because he was crying), I think he missed a much larger point. The boy came to his father for help and was taught that "men don't cry." The child apparently puffed out his chest and ran back to play with his friends. To the American male this is apparently a "happy ending." But it's not, really. Such attitudes teach future fathers to have emotional lives characterized by distance, separation, and alienation.

Jan recalls her grandparents very well. Her grandmother was full of life and laughter, her emotions easy to read and ever-flowing. Her grandfather was more stoic, like an old tree, silent and unmoving. He never hugged anyone or talked about his feelings. At his wife's funeral he was stiff and numb. He had nothing to say and seemed to endure, rather than welcome, the support he was given by friends and family. Going fishing alone was his solution to his loss.

Jan thinks her father was just like his dad. Communication in her family was always through her mother. "It was as if caring conversation was like the laundry," she said. "It was the mother's job." If her dad had any feelings on a matter, "he would have Mom call us and share his perspective."

Over the last few years, Jan has challenged her father to have a direct relationship with her. It hasn't come easy.

"At first he was surprised that it meant so much to me," she said. She reports that conversation between the two of them hasn't come easy, but that progress is being made. "Last week I hugged him good-bye and he hugged me back a little." That hug was obviously only a small thing, but it represented a great leap forward in that father-daughter relationship. And that father is much better off thanks to his daughter's persistence at working on their relationship.

Roger Axtell tells some fascinating stories about how men act in other cultures, stories that illustrate the American male's difficulties when it comes to showing affection.

On my first trip to the Middle East, my Arab business contact and I toured the city, walking along the street. He wore his long robe, the air was hot and dusty, a priest chanted the call to prayers from a nearby minaret, and I felt as far away from my American home as one could possibly be. At that moment, my business friend reached over, took my hand in his, and we continued walking along, his hand holding mine. . . .

Probably because I was so stunned, the one thing I didn't do was pull my hand away. I later learned that if I had jerked my hand out of his, I could have committed a Sahara-sized *faux pas*. In his country, this act of taking my hand in his was a sign of great friendship and respect.[1]

Throughout Latin America, Axtell explains that conversants tend to stand much closer together than Americans, and may literally stand toe to toe, placing their hands on the other person's arm or lapel.

Americans claim it takes years of experience, steely resolve, to stand that close and smell that many breaths. Some observers in Latin America even have a name for this charade. They call it "the conversational tango." That's the "dance" done by an American or European freshly arrived in Latin America who is confronted by this sudden and startling custom of closeness. The first reaction of the visitor is to step backward. But the Latin will soon follow. And so it goes, in a poorly choreographed tango. As one observer put it, "The dance only stops when the American is backed into a corner."[2]

Some cultures are very tolerant of physical contact; others are highly reserved. In American culture, most men are trained to avoid any demonstration of emotion. Understanding that your father was socialized to believe it is correct for a man to be unaffectionate may help you realize why he has had trouble showing affection to you.

2. How fathers were taught to discipline

For a very long time there has been a teaching in many cultures that a child is basically an "infant fiend."[3] I suspect the parent who first coined this term had a child with a hyperactivity disorder. Such children are generally spanking-resistant and can reduce a parent to putty unless properly treated. But in the old days, many families knew only the belt or the rod, and the philosophy of child rearing was that "a child needs to have his will crushed." Many parents believed that more spanking was better than less, and a father who was unsure of the best way to handle a situation could resort to "a good licking."

This model of child rearing has deep roots. In the early seventeenth century, John Robinson remarked that "surely there is in all children, though not alike, a stubbornness, and stoutness of mind arising from natural pride, which must, in the first place, be broken and beaten down; so that the foundation of their education being laid in humility and tractableness, other virtues may, in their time, be built thereon."[4]

Why do I raise this point? Simply because many fathers were raised in homes in which obedience was absolute. If they were disobedient—even in a minor matter—they would be beaten severely. Many fathers who treat their children brutally are simply reflecting what was modeled in their own childhoods.

Of course, this is not always easy to recognize. Mildred, a woman in her twenties, told me that her father's parents were "very special." She was certain they had no role in her own father's abusiveness. And it is true that sometimes a parent's abusive behavior has nothing at all to do with the way his parents treated him. And yet, we also need to realize that grandparents have done a great deal of changing by the time they have reached their older years. A father who, in his twenties, is under constant fear of losing his job and struggling to pay the bills will look very different when he is seventy and retired. According to Mildred, her grandfather used to calmly bounce a grandchild on his knee and laugh while he watched TV. The real issue, however, is not the way things are now, but rather what her father learned about "fathering" from him, when both were so many decades younger, in a very distant time and place.

A year later, in family therapy, Mildred's father revealed being "spanked" with a metal belt buckle when he was disobedient as a child. And so, Mildred's life shows us that our own family legacies and problems are sometimes difficult to discern.

3. Was your father trained to see children as parental slaves?

Many families have a long history of abusing children by "burning them out." Specifically, this can include expecting excess work from them and stealing their opportunity to be children, and expecting them to care for a parent (emotionally or materially). This type of behavior may be found in some families for more than a hundred years, perpetuated through three or four generations.

People who slaved for their parents when they were children often expect their own kids to do the same for them. Perhaps this is what is happening with one West Virginia farm child, a fourteen-year-old, who says: "I ain't going to stay here much longer; I have to work myself to death and don't get nothing out of it; never get to go *nowhurs*. I don't like it and I ain't goin' to stay."[5] I suspect that his father was worked hard by *his* parents, and was merely expecting the same from his son.

In the early part of the twentieth century, the practice of working children became so bad that the number of children under fifteen years of age who were working reached "almost two million—no doubt an undercount."[6] It was then that the government finally stepped in and passed a series of child labor laws. The laws were necessary because many parents believed they could use their children any way they wanted if it served their purposes. It was an assumption that many of our fathers were taught to believe because they lived it.

---

4. Fathers as breadwinners and mothers as nurturers

In the early days of this country, most fathers worked near their children. Farmer fathers plowed while their wives prepared meals; blacksmiths hammered horseshoes while their wives made clothing; carpenters swung hammers while their wives toted the laundry to the creek. Husbands and wives (and children) worked together for the common good of the family. Male and female often had different jobs, but both spouses usually "worked."

That all changed, however, with the advent of the industrial age. Men left their homes and went off to work in factories and foundries. After working long hours, they had little energy left to nurture anyone but themselves, and dragged themselves to bars, billiard halls, bowling alleys, and fraternal organizations.[7] If they were not quite meeting the financial needs of the family, then avoiding home was a way of avoiding their "failure."

With the advent of the Great Depression, the unemployment rate was approximately 25 percent, and jobless men began abandoning their families in record numbers, running from their powerlessness and disgrace and the hostility of their hungry families. Many ran because they could not handle their perceived failures.

Other men in the middle class survived, but in the decades that followed, the expectations of the family continued to rise, and consumerism grew steadily, requiring a man to provide more and more in order to be regarded as a "good father."

For example, a colleague told me he has taken on a second job. The reason? He has two children in private college and one in law school. Recently, his daughter called to tell her parents about her engagement. Her mother was home to share in her daughter's delight, while her father was working late at his office. Is this how it was with your family? Was your mother the nurturer? Was she the one who was available to talk (and to listen) while Dad worked long hours? Many of my patients say this is the culture they have known for three generations—like dominoes falling into the same pattern one generation after another.

142

---

5. Who taught your father how to father?

While there have always been people around to offer advice on parenting skills, many men in the earlier part of this century had minimal exposure to them. Most men were too busy working long hours trying to keep the family afloat financially. They just didn't think of "parenting" as important, nor did they realize the impact for good or bad they could have on their children. In this way, parenting is much like marriage. In our culture, one can go to school for twelve years and never get a course on either parenting or marriage. And so, when a culture does not stress the importance of fathering techniques, it is communicating that good fathering is not a respected goal in that culture. Men are trained to believe it is not a critical responsibility.

A few years ago, I heard a powerful illustration of a father's inability to appreciate his influence on his children. A speaker told of a congressman who had spent the day fishing with his son. Later that day he wrote in his diary, "Today, I went fishing with my son. A day wasted." The congressman's son also kept a diary; his notation for the same day read, "Went fishing with my father today—the greatest day of my life."

What do you think the congressman had on his mind when he was out fishing? He was probably thinking about all the work he had to do. Did he realize that his son was in the midst of the "greatest day" of his life? Apparently not.

Bob Pierce, the founder of World Vision, a relief organization that pours millions of dollars into worldwide relief for suffering children every year, was a man who failed to understand the degree to which he was needed by his own children.

Millions of children throughout the world have been rescued from poverty, hunger, and disease because Bob Pierce could not stand to see a child suffer. Yet he did not seem to understand that his own children also needed him desperately. During one of his trips to Vietnam, his daughter Sharon called and pleaded with him to come home. He attempted to reason with her, citing his responsibilities; he made no effort to change his plans. Sharon, however, was quite ill emotionally and wound up attempting suicide. Years later, another daughter, Marilee Pierce Dunker, offered praise for her father's work but lamented his ignorance about fathering. Her unfulfilled longing to know her father has left a void in her life. Therefore, her message to fathers is a simple one: "You are needed and important to your children—be available to them. Work and service are important, but not at the sacrifice of your children."[8] Unfortunately, many men have not heard her message in time to build healthy relationships with their children.

---

6. Training children for the "real world"

A child can't live at home with his parents forever. Sooner or later he needs to leave the nest.

But the way an adolescent is trained to leave home can significantly affect his or her relationship with Dad. Some children are encouraged to stay too long; consequently, the transition from dependence to independence is stunted, and perhaps never completed. Other children are pushed out of the nest too early; they often end up with broken wings—overwhelmed, rejected, or hurt.

Learning how this process occurred in past generations of your family is an important step to understanding. If your father curtly announced, "When you're eighteen, you're out on the street," you may wonder if that is how his father sent him into "the world." A father may fear that his child will get so comfortable at home that he will never grow up. Some fathers wonder if their children will be able to handle the challenges of life. They say, "Life is rough, so I'll be rough on you to prepare you," or, "I learned by being on my own, by struggling to survive, and now you must learn the same tough lessons." Yet, some fathers give the opposite message, "Live here forever." Such fathers may have lived at home until they were in their late twenties or early thirties, feeling no urgency to leave, and even giving their paychecks to their parents to manage. These fathers do not understand their children's needs for independence, and may not prepare them properly for adulthood.

Guiding an older adolescent or young adult in the process of leaving home is a tenuous event, with errors on both sides. Getting a glimpse of it may at least help you identify problems in your own "leaving" experience.

144

7. Changing cultural patterns promote father alienation

Many adult children have found it a powerful exercise to go back and look at their father's life. I realize that this is not possible for everyone, but it is good if you can delve back into your father's and grandfather's youths. Doing this may not dissolve your legitimate issues and differences with your father, but it will enhance your understanding. Taking a look at your cultural genealogy will give you more insight into your father's world and help you evaluate what you want to change and do differently in your own life.

Looking back at your father's (or grandfather's) life, you may find a number of reasons why "father alienation" has increased. For example, the transfer of a family from one culture to another—such as from Europe to America—often involves increased alienation. The father may want to preserve the old culture, while the children are ashamed of it.

New technology offers new types of work, which means that fewer children follow in their father's footsteps. Better educated youths may find it hard to relate to poorly educated parents. These are just some of the ways a genealogy can help explain why you have such different perspectives—by showing the different worlds you and your father have experienced.

Understanding your father is a very important step in the process of improving your relationship with him for a number of reasons. It allows you to mix empathy with confrontation so you can successfully make changes in your relationship. For example, "Dad, I know you and your father showed closeness by playing cards together, but I would enjoy it more if we could talk about where we are emotionally." Understanding your father gives you insight into your own life—ways you blindly endorsed his values or reactively opposed them, merely because they were his. And finally, understanding your father may create empathy.

For some, however, empathy for a father who hurt them so severely is virtually impossible. The fact that they can articulate their anger is probably a good thing—at least it's better than denying the anger and pretending all is well. An understanding of anger, bitterness, and confrontation skills is critical for all relationships, but sometimes especially so with a father.

16

Dealing with Anger and Healing the Pain

● ●

*A*nger is deadly.
It kills the mind, the soul, *and* the body.

Years ago I read an intriguing story about synthetic gems that radiated with an amazing luminescence. They were so appealing to the eye that they enchanted anyone who held them. But there was one rather major drawback: They emitted radiation that slowly killed anyone who kept them—a slight bug in the design left by their creator. They passed from person to person, perhaps even being stolen a couple of times, and slowly proved fatal to each charmed owner.

That's the way it is with anger. It is hard for someone who has been wronged—particularly if it was by someone they trusted (like a father)—to let go of anger. There is a satisfaction that comes from feeling "righteous indignation" and from fantasizing about getting even. But it is a spirit-killing kind of satisfaction from which nothing good can come.

Those who harbor anger or resentment against a father (living or dead) are causing untold injury—not to their fathers but to themselves.

So what do we do with this anger? How do we break its hold on us? How can we stop what anger does to us?

"It's easy," some well-meaning Christian might say. "Just forgive."

But it is not helpful for a person to "forgive and forget" before he has been able to work through his pain. Such forgiveness may be no forgiveness at all. That person may merely try to stuff things down inside, or be made to feel that his feelings of anger are "wrong," and so he engages in what I call "magic forgiveness"—a quick, positive wish to make the rage go away. Nothing is confronted or dealt with.

Dealing with Anger toward Your Father

1. Forgiveness is not the same as trust[1]

I have seen fathers (who have hurt their families deeply) turn their lives around and become decent, caring fathers. Such a process usually takes years, depending on the father's starting place. When this happens, some adult children are afraid of forgiveness because they believe, "If I forgive my father, we'll have to act like nothing happened. And then he may hurt me again." This is a legitimate concern, but it mixes apples and oranges. Forgiveness does not mean that you have to pretend as if you trust your father again. Trust is not a right anyone can demand. It is something that emerges over time from stable, reliable relationships. If your father has abused you, the best road to take is usually the slow one. "I'm feeling rushed and overwhelmed" is a legitimate answer if you are feeling hurried in the reconciliation process. The fact that you are even willing to engage in an attempt at reconciliation with your father is to your credit.

2. Understand that it's okay to express your anger

Last month I had an emergency that caused me to arrive twenty-five minutes late for an appointment. My patient was quite upset because he had important issues to discuss, and he let me know how he felt—in no uncertain terms. After I picked my eardrums off the floor, I apologized. Since then, we have been able to continue our work. Why did I tell you this story? Because I wanted you to see that it was important that I let my patient share his frustration *fully* before I apologized. I wanted to be sure that my apology was meant to bring healing, and not merely intended to shut him down before he had a chance to express how he felt.

Did you ever get mad at someone and have him apologize before you even got ten words out of your mouth? In such cases the irritation is often left inside you because the other person has made you feel that you're wrong to be angry. What's wrong is shutting a person down with an apology and then communicating, "Hey, I said I was sorry. What more do you want?"

It is dishonest—and often destructive to the relationship—to hide or deny feelings of anger. Striving for honest communication that is not too harsh is often the best policy.

3. Box in the offense

When someone has hurt you badly, you tend to begin disliking everything about him. For example, as you get in touch with your father's past offenses against you, you might even start resenting the color of his socks. Be prepared for that eventuality, and try to stick to the things that are at the heart of the problem. Don't make subtle, irritable quips and pick at him. It only makes you look irrational and unreasonable.

Also, try to avoid taking your "father annoyances" out on those who remind you of your father. If you're not extremely careful with your anger, it can become a free-floating kind of bitterness that will destroy relationships with people who mean you only good.

4. Do not allow further abuse from your father

In dealing with anger, healing of past offenses is extremely important. But so is the process of making sure that no new resentment is added on top of the old.

As my father and I began working on our relationship, he suggested that I was "letting things go" and stewing about them, and he was right.

"If you don't like something I'm doing or saying," he said, "tell me about it right then."

I took him at his word, even though most people would prefer to have any reproofs occur privately. The next time he said something that irritated me, I told him about it immediately. Amazingly, my challenge didn't seem to bother him at all, and I found myself without residual irritation. Today I can't even remember what I was upset about, and I think that says quite a bit about my father's wisdom.

Prevent further alienation by educating your father about what you like and don't like and be open to hearing about *your* habits or personality traits that annoy or anger him.

---

5. Don't expect your father to ask for your forgiveness

Sometimes a father will realize his mistakes and ask for his child's forgiveness. But that doesn't happen very often.

If you confront your father with his offenses, even if you do it graciously, he may still feel threatened. For your own sake, don't let your forgiveness hinge on your father's perfect response. You may tell your alcoholic father, "Dad, you have no idea how ashamed I was to bring my friends home when I was a kid . . . and it still hurts me that you have such a drinking problem." These words may need to be said, but don't expect them to go over very well.

You need to forgive whether your father wants forgiveness or not. After all, you forgive partly for yourself, to free your own emotions and thoughts from tormenting, bitter fantasies.

---

6. Confide in someone

Some people say that it is wrong to share your anger with anyone other than the person with whom you're angry. They suggest that to confide in a therapist, for example, is "gossip." This is silly, of course; even the apostle Paul wrote bluntly about the abuse he received from many people. If you have faced serious abuse, working through it alone is probably impossible. You will need some trusted friends and a counselor to help process your healing. And if a father continues to hurt members of his family, showing no signs of changing his behavior, it may be appropriate—for the sake of your healing and the healing of your family—to discuss his problem with select family members.

---

7. Practice the process of forgiveness

I believe it was C. S. Lewis who said, "Forgiveness is like trying to quit smoking. I've tried it fifty times." What a true statement. Forgiveness is a process. You may need to forgive your father fifty times for the same offense. I recall an offense that once made me so angry that I had to pray two hours every day for a week to be released from my uncomfortable anger and rage. On the sixth day I woke up and could no longer find any hatred in my heart. It was gone.

So you see, forgiveness is not merely a man-made act. It is something that flows from the personality of our eternal Father. If his Spirit has been sent into your being, he has been joined with you and can empower you to forgive your father, just as you have been forgiven *by* your Father. It's a supernatural act, but that doesn't mean it will happen instantaneously.

8. Be patient with the process

One of the pitfalls of therapy is that people sometimes feel worse before they feel better. And some people fear that if they touch the grief of their father memories, they will be swallowed up by the pain and never escape.

But people's past experiences tend to hold only a finite amount of grief to be "worked through." It may take years—and much effort—but the process offers hope for a brighter tomorrow, no matter how dark the present may be. And there are techniques you can use, either alone or with a supportive counselor, to facilitate healing. And there are three things *you* need to help you prepare to deal with the hurt you feel:

- A safe place in which you can recover and be restored
- Some time to lean, rather than lead
- Commitment to deal with any anger, fear, or guilt you feel concerning your father

Dealing with the Loss of Your Father

Do you ever imagine yourself having a conversation with your father, even though he has been dead for a year or more? Are you unable to face anniversaries or his old possessions without profound emotions? Do you avoid any discussion about him? Do you talk about his death with cold stoicism? If your answers to such questions are yes, then you may still need to work through your painful memories. Only after you have finished grieving the past will you be able to live happily and healthily in the present—especially if your father's death left unresolved conflicts and emotions between you.

First of all, exposing yourself to your emotions is a powerful healing tool. Many therapists believe that what you don't verbalize and talk through, you will deal with by "acting out." Adult acting out can take many forms, including binge shopping, excess eating, abusing alcohol, self-destructive sexuality, or compulsive exercise.

Some losses can be dealt with by simply talking through the pain with a close friend, sibling, or spouse. Some may call for the support of a pastoral counselor, minister, priest, or rabbi, and other losses may require therapy on a more extended basis. In every situation, however, grief work should include talking with someone you trust.

Generally, the goal is to allow for modest amounts of pain to be expressed in each session—like bursts of air from a balloon. If you feel the process is going too fast and you are uncomfortable, say so. Occasionally, over-eager therapists move too quickly for the pain. If this is the case in your situation, tell your therapist the pace you can handle.

If you meet with a trained counselor, he or she might employ special techniques to help you get in touch with your pain.

For example, a therapist might employ a "two-chair technique," in which you are urged to talk to an empty chair in his or her office, pretending your father is there.

Others may assist you in creating imagined meetings with your father. Mary Cerney, a psychologist affiliated with the Menninger Association, writes of the experience of "Susan."[2] Susan's father was an alcoholic who eventually quit drinking, but who continued to abuse and terrorize his family. When Susan was twelve, her parents divorced. Her mother eventually remarried, and life in the family settled down.

However, after a time, Susan's younger sister Janet began to fight with her mother, and so eventually went to live with her father. After six months, Janet and her mother reconciled, and her father said that he would drive the girl back home to her mother's house. On the trip home, a drunk driver hit their car; both Janet and her father were killed.

For more than two years after this tragic event, Susan had trouble sleeping, and she had constant nightmares about her father that began to affect her waking hours. In the nightmares her father would want to talk to her (something he rarely wanted to do in real life), and he looked like a corpse, with a severely damaged arm from the accident.

Dr. Cerney changed the dream through the use of guided imagery. She helped Susan re-access the picture of her father stored in her memory, and to begin to master the memory. She touched her father's corpse-like face and damaged arm, and they were "healed." Susan had an imaginary dialogue with her father in which she shared her irritations, anger, and love for him. She discussed their relationship and told him all about the ways he had hurt her. She also asked him how he felt about her stepfather, and had him answer that he was glad she was now receiving the love she had always wanted from him. When there was nothing left to ask or say, Susan saw—in her mind's eye—her father smiling. Then he walked over, hugged her, and waved good-bye. Susan's nightmares stopped because she resolved several issues with her father; she had closure.

Guided imagery takes many forms. One popular form, which can be quite effective, invites God's fatherhood and strength into the memories and trauma and loss, so that an experience suffered in orphan aloneness is now re-experienced in the presence and with the comfort of God.

Some counselors may encourage you to do "homework" in which you write a letter to your father, telling him what you really feel about him and your relationship. In cases where the father is still alive, sometimes these letters are rewritten (to make them less hostile) and then are actually sent.

Other counselors have their patients write good-bye letters to their fathers who have died. Then, they may suggest burning the letters and scattering their ashes in a personally meaningful way. A pastoral counselor may suggest that such a letter be burned like incense that can rise up to God. Some might even have you pray that God the Father would communicate your feelings to your departed father.

A counselor may also suggest keeping a journal about your relationship with your father. A journal often accelerates insight, and putting thoughts on paper can help you deal with them. One middle-aged female patient of mine decided to journal about her father and just let her memories roll onto the page. Four hours later she had typed twenty-five pages. When we met for our next session, she had a great deal of new insight into her relationship with her father.

For some clients, being exposed to the places and images of their fathers helps them grieve. Wearing his coat, his ties, his rings, or looking at old home movies or photos can spur expression and bring healing.

Another healing technique is to write your father's eulogy. A eulogy allows you to process your father's life in terms of the impact he has had on your life.

I am sometimes asked if it is possible to grieve through music, poetry, or artwork. In other words, can creativity heal emotional pain? I am inclined to answer that sharing your longings and father pains through your creative outlets often gives you extra enthusiasm for your craft and should be encouraged. And yet such outlets are often insufficient and can promote excessive isolation—the songwriter who grieves through songs written in private may be too comfortable with coping styles that promote withdrawal.

However, during times of loss and grief, it is helpful to immerse yourself in creative beauty. Pain can convince you that life is meager and not particularly fulfilling, so make sure your eyes are open to beauty of all types. During such times it is good to experience a taste of heaven: appealing music, a massage, a bike ride, laughter with a silly friend, a good book, or anything else that soothes you.

You may also find comfort in a support group. A support group can provide you with innumerable benefits. It can give you a sense of safety and belonging, an understanding that others feel the same way and accept your honest feelings. It can be a place to see your usefulness to others and where they can help you, too. There are many types of support groups, so you should have no trouble finding one that's right for you.

Be careful to find a group that does more than engage in discussions about information, but also offers support and encouragement. If you are working through some serious father issues, you are going to need more than cold, hard data to be healed.

It Might Be Chemical

Finally, I should note that prolonged grief can be due to biochemical problems that make it very hard for the brain to process a loss. It is common for those with biological vulnerabilities to show their first serious depression after a crisis. Friends and family members see their loved one going through all sorts of changes—weight loss, loss of appetite, persistent fatigue—and they think, "This is just a stage he has to go through. It's nothing to be alarmed about."

Sometimes, though, it *is* something to be alarmed about, and something that requires prompt treatment. I regularly receive referrals from trained counselors that I should have received months earlier, but didn't, because those counselors were slow to recognize the signs of a biological depression. If you notice that you are stuck in the grieving process and have new weight, sleep, or appetite changes (increased or decreased), poor concentration, hopelessness, agitation, physical slowness, inappropriate guilt, or a loss of interest in your hobbies, then get a psychiatric evaluation. Some people have been walking around in a state of emotional crisis for years, simply because no one ever had them checked out to see if it might be a medical problem.

After you have confronted your pain and begun the healing process, you may feel a new sense of strength. With new emotional resources, you may find the ability to begin to rebuild and restore your relationship with your father. After the pain comes the payoff.

17

Maximizing Your Father Relationship

• •

*S*teven is the son of a farmer, the second of four children. It was not until his first child was born that he began to think more about his own childhood.

He began to reflect on his childhood experiences of being hit by his father for coming home late or for touching the man's prized stereo equipment. The more he remembered, the angrier he became. Occasionally he would drive alone and scream about these past events, about the constant yelling and fighting that had taken place between his parents. Finally, he decided that he needed to discuss these memories and work them through with a counselor.

After eighteen months in counseling, Steven decided to talk with his father about their past. He wrote his father a letter, explaining that he wanted to be closer, but that he needed to get some things off his chest. He described many of his earliest memories: being chased around the house, being jabbed in the abdomen with a broom handle, and being punched in the arms and chest. He was very firm in saying that this method of discipline was abusive and that he felt his father owed him an apology.

Steven didn't simply send this letter to his father; he also sent copies to his two sisters and brother. Later he realized that even though he was forty years old, he was still acting like a scared child, trying to reduce his fear by enlisting the support of his siblings. His brother, Rich, immediately agreed with the contents of the letter and described his own bitterness with their father. His sister Meg, although their father's favorite, had always been the one who would scream whenever Steven was beaten, asking their father to stop. She called her brother and said through tears that she was sorry he had such hurtful memories. She could never speak ill of their father, but did offer her sincere understanding and love.

Steven was feeling pretty good about things until his father called with his reaction to the letter. Unfortunately, he was more upset over the fact that Steven had sent the letter to his siblings than by the content of the letter itself. He was embarrassed, and that was all that seemed to matter to him—not that he and his son had some major differences that needed to be worked out.

"Hey," he told Steven, "I was the one who always defended you in front of the other family members. I've always been in your corner. I always told 'em you were a good kid."

Steven was surprised at his father's reactivity. As he thought about it, however, he realized that he should have expected such a reaction. His father just wasn't any good at expressing his feelings; perhaps he didn't even know what his feelings were.

He wound up deciding to invite his father to his personal counseling sessions, hoping that his father's participation would help them both. But it didn't work out that way—at least not at first. His father came to the next session, but he seemed nervous and afraid, and proceeded to explain to the counselor why Steven had so many problems.

"The boy never did relate well to us," he began. "We never understood why. We would go to the mountains to camp, and he never wanted to come. He was an accident, you know, but I tried to love him and treat him well anyway. He could never relate."

Because the counselor wanted to build a rapport with Steven's father, Ben, he didn't interrupt the man's monologue, and Steven was unsure how to respond to his father's words. Part of him wondered, "Why wouldn't I relate to my family? That does seem odd of me." But another part was thinking, "Listen to his denial; he is deflecting the whole goal of this session!"

The following week, Steven and his dad met for a second session, during which Steven repeated his desire that they improve their relationship. Ben said that he was open to getting closer, but then blamed his son for the fact that they weren't close. "I've been reaching out to you for years," he said. "What do you want from me?"

The counselor could see that Ben was threatened and felt attacked by any hint that he might need to change, so he asked the man about his relationship with his own father.

"My father and I were soul mates," he began. "We were very close. We never needed to talk about how we felt 'cause we just knew."

"How often did you and your father talk after you grew up?"

"Not much, really. Maybe once every two or three months. He wasn't big on writing or telephoning. Being a farmer, he always had a lot to do. He would visit us twice a year until he was seventy-five, which is when he died in a car accident."

"That must have been very painful for you."

"Oh, that's true," Ben agreed. "It was the last time I cried. Yes, he was a wonderful man—better than me."

"What do you mean?" the counselor asked.

"He just did a lot of good things for a lot of people. When he died, there were hundreds and hundreds of cars that drove down the road to that church. Everybody liked him. Everybody."

"And what did you guys do to be so close?"

"Well . . . we competed against each other. We'd go to the local tavern and shoot pool. And believe me, we played for blood. But really, I loved to see him win."

"Did you ever talk about your feelings for each other?"

"Not directly. But we didn't need to. When we battled in the pool hall you could feel it."

As Steven drove home that night, he thought about his father's behavior. He was both frustrated and pleased. He was frustrated because every time he reached out to his father, the man did something to sabotage things. He was also annoyed at his father's competitiveness, his attempts to control the sessions, and the way he romanticized *his* father.

At the same time, however, he was pleased to learn about some of the patterns of the past. He was struck by his father's belief that games were the foundation to "real intimacy," and that talk was more of an act to be endured, not a necessary ingredient for closeness. Such insight helped Steven gain a new understanding of his relationship with his father.

Eventually, both men elected to invite Steven's mother to join the sessions. She was happy to come because she thought this was her chance to get her husband "fixed." However, Steven and his mother quickly began to talk between themselves and Ben withdrew into the corner. He could not compete with the emotional fluency of his wife. The counselor tried to get Ben back into the conversation, but he would quickly back out and let his wife talk on his behalf.

Whenever he did speak up, it was usually to argue with his wife rather than to talk to his son. After a few such sessions, Ben began finding reasons not to attend the counseling sessions.

Finally, Steven talked him into coming back to the sessions with the stipulation that it would be just the two of them. Steven recognized that when his mother was involved in their counseling sessions, she and Ben spent the time focusing on their own problems (which was necessary, but which detracted from the real purpose of the sessions—namely, to restore the father-son relationship).

Steven and his dad are still in counseling, and they are beginning to spend more time with each other away from their therapist's office. They are learning about each other, slowly, carefully, but they are beginning to take steps in the right direction.

Lessons from Ben and Steven

Several lessons can be drawn from the story of Steven and his father about father-child relationships.

1. You can't force the issue

Steven's intention in sending a letter to his father was to get an apology. He thought, *Either he will apologize and admit his failure or he'll never see me again. I'm tired of pretending I've been blind to his abuses.* Unfortunately, his approach almost undermined the reconciliation he sought. His letter was intense and confrontational, it was bound to intimidate his father. The letter was basically a challenge: "Either apologize to me or get out of my life."

Reconciliation can't be forced.

2. Healing doesn't come in a moment

Steven had a couple of fantasies about healing his relationship with his father. He imagined his father receiving his letter and being overcome with insight; he envisioned Ben seeing the abusiveness of his past behavior and becoming so remorseful that he would come to Steven and ask, through tears, for forgiveness. The two men would end up being close friends after this—laughing, joking, and generally enjoying each other's company.

Steven also fantasized that, if his father resisted and fought the truth, the entire family would join the battle, collectively getting Ben to admit his failures as a father and bringing about an immediate change in his behavior.

In both fantasies, the healing of the relationship occurred within days—moments, really. In reality, efforts to rebuild a troubled relationship generally take months to years. There may be large breakthroughs along the way, but it takes time to arrive at the quality of relationship Steven wants. In some cases, only small improvements are possible—not every father has the ability to develop mature closeness with his child.

3. Reactive dialogue doesn't help

Steven was amazed at how much trouble his father had with mature conversation. It seemed that his father's communication repertoire was limited to withdrawal, accusation, or talk about third parties. Sharing his own personal feelings was frightening. When Ben began to feel guilty or uncomfortable, he would become loud and reactive, and Steven would have to say, "Dad . . . you're yelling!" Ben always seemed surprised, as if he had been totally unaware of the increasing loudness of his voice.

Loud, reactive dialogue can sabotage the process of healing and reconciliation. Slow, careful communication is easier to handle and less threatening.

4. The value (and danger) of joint counseling sessions

The goal of Steven and Ben's sessions together should have been to work on overcoming the estrangement between father and son. Both should have come for themselves, not as servants of the other. Instead, Ben came to help out Steven, which only served to infantilize and emasculate his son, as if he said, "I am a dutiful, healthy father who is going to sacrifice his precious time to help his sick, sick son." It was quickly apparent that Ben never would have come to counseling at all unless it was "to help Steven." It would have been too threatening for him to admit that he himself needed help with emotional problems.

Joint counseling sessions can be very valuable *if* both parties are genuinely seeking to get out of the sessions what is best for them.

5. The question of who should pay for the sessions

Steven paid for the earliest sessions with his father, but he began to feel that doing so was an additional sign that he was a "loser." He interpreted the act of paying to mean that he was the one in need, and his father was the benevolent sacrificial guest. He would think, "He beat me up every other week for years, and I'm the one who has problems? I don't think so." His feelings were right, and although Ben was reluctant at first, he finally agreed to pay half the cost of the sessions.

6. Deciding whether other family members should come

When Steven's mother, Ann, came to the sessions, she helped *and* hindered the process. Because she knew both men, she was able to confirm and correct their perspectives. However, she soon began to speak on behalf of her husband to express his feelings for him. Ben soon withdrew because his wife had "taken over." When she stepped in, Ben stepped out.

Ben and his wife also allowed the conversation to turn repeatedly to their marriage, although the purpose of the sessions was to help Steven develop a better relationship with his father. Unfortunately, Ben and Ann repeatedly raised personal marriage strengths with the therapist in order to communicate that they were a good and loving couple who were just there for their son. The therapist repeatedly had to redirect the focus of the discussion to the purpose of the sessions. Further, talk between Ben and Ann let Ben momentarily escape the scarier task of being intimate with his son.

7. Continuing your therapy alone

After a time of counseling with his father, Steven began to feel that he was becoming insecure again. He became less sure of himself at work, and was more sensitive to teasing comments from his staff. He felt as if he was losing ground.

He discussed these feelings with his counselor, and they decided that the introduction of Steven's parents into the counseling room had undermined the "safeness" Steven had previously enjoyed. The man who had repeatedly beaten him when he was a child was now intimidating him in the counseling center. And even though Ben had been invited, Steven was expecting things to move faster.

Steven and his therapist decided to begin having extra sessions without Steven's parents, to deal with the pressure of working through Steven's personal issues: his work, his relationships with others, and his dealings with his father.

8. When your father puts you back in diapers

Steven was often frustrated because his father treated him like a child. He even called him "Stevie" during one of the counseling sessions. It was hard for Ben to imagine that his son could be better than him at anything. Ben spoke with pride of Steven's work as a writer and editor, but he was unable to see his son as a fellow adult when they spoke alone.

Fathers often fail to make the transition to an adult relationship with their adult children. It may be necessary to remind your father that even though you are the child and he is the parent, you are both adults now, and should relate on an equal basis.

9. Handling two common avoidance techniques

When Steven finally was able to talk face to face with his father about events that upset him, Ben did two things to deflect the issue. He said he wanted "to leave the past behind," and at other times Ben would talk about his own pain when Steven confronted him. Why is this avoidance so important?

First, Steven's abuses occurred in the past, and that is where much of his emotional energy still resides. Ben's devaluation of the past makes Steven out to be strange—"Why live in that past rut?" It is a failure in empathy and hinders healing.

Further, when Ben talks about his trials immediately after being confronted by Steven, it makes Steven out to be a sadist—as if he is picking on his poor, overburdened father when he holds him accountable for past errors.

Shirley's Story

Shirley was the strong-willed child of missionary parents. Early in her life, her father—using a combination of God, the Bible, the church, and physical and emotional abuse—convinced her that everything inside her was black and sinful and that to feel good about herself was a sign of arrogance and pride.

He never taught me that I was made in the image of God, that God loved me in my humanness. I thought you had to be perfect or God would withhold his love and affection—just like my father.

My father firmly believed in corporal punishment . . . [but he] had not merely used spanking to control and break me—he had used physical abuse. He had cut twigs from the trees outside our home and beat us on our bare skin. The beatings always left thick welts and sometimes even drew blood. . . .

In my early thirties I began to feel tremendous rage toward my father, God, and organized religion in general. Obviously, I was angry over the physical abuse, but I also began to see the emotional abuse caused by my father and the legalistic teachings of my church. I saw what legalism had done to my self-esteem, and to my sense of identity, and that I had developed a self-loathing. I saw the wreckage in my mind and emotions—a happy childhood lost forever.

Over the next five years, I struggled with a great deal of resentment toward my parents, particularly my father. During this crisis period, my father was also doing some re-evaluating. He truly became aware of the magnitude of his mistakes and made several gestures toward apologizing for the past. . . .

In my head I accepted his apologies, but in my heart I continued to keep him at a distance. Perhaps I wanted to pay him back for the years of emotional pain his defective parenting had caused me—perhaps because it was too scary to think about being close to him. At this stage of my life I didn't really want a relationship with my father. My anger had become an important part of my identity. I had not merely been victimized, I had defined myself as a "victim." In my mind I had created a polarized scenario of my childhood, in which I was the good and healthy child and everyone else was sick. Now I see this as a simplistic, distorted image of my family, but it became firmly entrenched in my psyche for a number of years. And as the victim survivor and "good" member of the family, I needed only to look out and accuse, without looking in and rebuilding my fragmented heart. My image of my family enabled me to avoid looking at my own issues. . . .

At this point, my own children were getting close to adolescence and it was becoming increasingly clear to me that nothing is black and white. I began to see that I had probably been a very challenging child to rear—to put it mildly. As I was forced to rear a strong-willed child of my own, I felt my emotions often pushed to the edge. Experiences such as these began to erode my polarized picture of the past. The blacks and whites of my childhood began to merge into a more realistic gray. I began to see my father as a mere human being.

And so it was that one day, several years ago, I went to my father and told him that I was sorry for my attitude toward him over the years . . . [and] for the resentment that I had carried toward him throughout my adulthood.

My father . . . listened very quietly and when I had finished speaking he said simply, "This completes things for me." And the core of anger that I had been building inside for years rolled apart. At that moment in time, I finally forgave my father for the past. My father is not a verbally expressive man, but in his own uncertain way, he expressed to me how much my words had healed our relationship. All these years I had waited for him to say or do something that would heal the wound inside me. I had ignored all his many past attempts to befriend me. I had not realized that the missing piece was my change of heart.

Today we enjoy a real closeness as father and daughter. I can hug him with genuine warmth. When we speak on the telephone, I'm talking to my father, my friend. The resentment that I carried around with me for so many years has evaporated. There are no more barriers in my relationship with him. I'm free to both give him love and receive love from him.

Shirley offers us a number of useful observations and key principles of reconciliation. In her youth she smothered her own feelings and wanted to appease her father's anger. What she felt and wanted was irrelevant. The only thing important was learning how to keep safe from her father's rage. To survive, she embraced his beliefs but grew to despise them in her early adulthood. As an adult she developed insight into how the abuse was controlling and limiting her identity. She realized that acknowledging the reality and impact of what her father had done did not mean she had to define herself in terms of his mistakes. She could take the abuse very seriously without changing her name to "Shirley Abused." She also realized that her resentment had progressively expanded beyond the bounds of her father. It poisoned her toward anything or anyone who reminded her of him. Eventually, she was able to see that her father had made mistakes simply because he was a human being, just as she was. He had struggled as a parent, just as she did. Finally, she was able to deal with her past, accept that her father had grown, and receive his love.

The Value of a Mentor

Unfortunately, not all attempts at reconciliation end so well, and even successful attempts may be incomplete. For some a 20 percent improvement in the relationship can be true success and have a healing impact. Hearing a father say he is not able or willing to do further reconciliation work can be healing. It takes the pressure off you and leaves it with the parent. Fathers often cannot be all that their children need due to their own emotional and physical limitations. There is, however, another reason for limits in the father-child relationship. Adult children often differ radically from their fathers; they pursue different careers, hobbies, interests, and possess different personality styles. That is why sometimes, even as a father-child relationship improves, it is still valuable to develop a relationship with a caring, fatherly mentor.

A mentor might be a loving uncle, coach, teacher, sage, protector, wise guide, facilitator,[1] sponsor, older brother, older friend, or counselor.

Mentor relationships have been praised for millennia. When Odysseus went on his ten-year journey, he entrusted his son to an old man named Mentor, who ended up saving the boy's life.[2] Since then, history has celebrated mentoring relationships between Socrates and Plato, Lorenze de Medici and Michelangelo, Haydn and Beethoven, Freud and Jung, Boas and Mead.[3]

A mentor does not have to be an older, more powerful man who acts in the role of the sage, however. A mentor might be any man or woman who is strong in an area in which you are weak. Many of my patients are older than I am. If they were not open to my counsel, they would be wasting their time. If they are able to accept my guidance, even though I am younger, they usually can be helped.

How can you find a mentor? Let me suggest a few places to look:

- Your family—older brothers, uncles, older cousins, grandfathers
- Your spouse's family—Moses' father-in-law was a wise mentor
- Your father's friends and friends of older relatives
- Older employers or employees
- Ministers, elders, priests, and rabbis

If you search such fields without finding any fruit, let me suggest some steps you can take to develop a pool of possible mentors:

- If you are in a church with a younger crowd, try visiting one where there's more gray hair.
- Start attending the fellowship groups, home groups, and so on of your church, where it might be easier to develop a one-on-one relationship with an older person.
- Participate in organizations that stress things that interest you.
- Attend classes taught by older professors.
- Use older individuals to provide services you need (accountants, gardeners, lawyers), and seek to learn from them.

Once you have found someone you think would be an excellent mentor, spend some time getting to know him or her; see if a personal chemistry develops between you. If you respect this person and enjoy his or her company, say so! Over time you will sense the quality and consistency of the friendship. Once you are confident that this person would make a good mentor, consider asking if he or she would be willing to mentor you.

Be prepared to be specific about what you expect of the relationship. Will you be meeting together once a week? Once a month? In person or over the phone? Will you meet for prayer and Bible study, or chat over coffee at a neighborhood restaurant? What do you want the relationship to accomplish for you? For your mentor?

If you would like more direction, consult Bobb Biehl and Glen Urquhart's booklet, *Mentoring: How to Find a Mentor and How to Become One.* You can order by writing MGI, P.O. Box 952499, Lake Mary, FL 32795-2499 or calling 1-800-443-1976.

Some Problems with Mentors

Problems may arise in mentoring relationships—as with any relationship—and you should be aware of these. For example, a mentor who wants to make you an extension of his personality is a poor choice. Someone who doesn't respect you or your capacity to think for yourself, who expects you to think as he does, doesn't understand the mentor role. A mentor should want to help you achieve *your* dreams—not *his* dreams.

Occasionally a mentor is resistant to his "mentee's" progress. He or she may feel threatened as the relationship changes, and you become more of an equal and less of a student. She may become critical and jealous; he may withdraw support or increase his paternal posturing. Such developments usually signal a dying relationship. A good mentor will welcome a pupil's growth and advancement as a compliment to his or her mentoring skills. In such a situation, the mentor may still offer support and guidance, but the student will become more confident of his or her own opinions—and may even make occasional suggestions to the mentor.

Another potential problem is the development of a romance between a mentor and his mentee. A common scenario has the older male mentor (who is often married) becoming sexually involved with a younger female pupil.

For this reason, if a woman seeks out only male mentors and not female ones, she should investigate why. A woman whose only supportive relationship is with her mentor is in a situation where loneliness and sexuality could easily mix and explode. Women who are victims of incest may be more vulnerable to repeating the act with their "fatherly" mentor if they have not worked out the abuse.[4] As with any victimization, there may be a compulsion to repeat it.

An awareness of the potential problems that can develop in a mentoring relationship can help ensure a supportive and successful association—one that can facilitate healing in other relationships.

Charles Stanley points out the value of mentoring relationships with a story from his own experience. As a boy, he had a kind Sunday school teacher named Craig Stowe, who pursued and loved Charles even after he switched churches. Stowe saw Charles every day as the boy sold newspapers on the street. He would pull over to ask Charles how he was doing, tell him that he was being prayed for, and buy a newspaper from him (always paying five times the price of the paper). Because he had no father or surrogate father to encourage him, young Charles Stanley was greatly affected by Craig Stowe's caring friendship. Today, he says he will always remember an important point: Giving a little bit to someone who has nothing is a very big deal.[5]

You may be waiting for a mentor to seek you out; or you may be ready to take the initiative to find a mentor. That's good. But why not reach out and meet someone else's needs, too? Why not find someone to teach and invest your life in? It just might change your life. And *theirs*.

18

The Everlasting Father

*W*hen Christ was baptized at the age of thirty, he heard a voice from heaven say, "You are my Son, whom I love; with you I am well pleased" (Luke 3:22). Those words empowered him as he began his ministry. He was coming to spread a truth that would turn the world upside down.

But notice what happened immediately after those words of love were spoken; he went out into the desert and was attacked with a temptation. And what was this first temptation? Cookies? A Mercedes? Sexual pleasure? An all-expenses-paid Caribbean cruise? No . . . it was an attack on the identity of Jesus. Satan said, "If you are the Son of God, tell this stone to become bread" (Luke 4:3).

The third temptation used the same opening phrase, "If you are the Son of God. . . ." Satan apparently was trying to raise doubt in Christ's mind about the accuracy of the words Jesus had just heard from his Father—that he is his Father's Son, and that his Father loves him. It appears that Satan likes nothing better than to see a child of God lose the identity and security he or she has in Christ. But you can remain strong and secure in your relationship with God no matter what is thrown at you. In this chapter I want to give you a few suggestions for maintaining and strengthening your parent-child relationship with your eternal Father.

It's easy to feel inadequate and insecure, especially when you compare yourself with God's purity or with the good things others have done.

Very few of us could favorably compare our lives to someone like Mother Teresa, for instance. But when you think that your relationship with the heavenly Father depends on the good things you're doing, you've forgotten that the whole point of Jesus' ministry and death on the cross was to die for our sins. In Jesus we have all won, and we all shine like Mother Teresa!

It is easy to forget the gospel. I sometimes go for days without confidence, and without that cherished feeling that only God can give me. The apostle Paul noted the same problem with the Christians living in Galatia; he asked them, "Who has stolen your joy?" Paul's question is pertinent today. I regularly meet people who need to hear Paul whispering down the hall of time, reminding them that they don't have to earn God's love and blessings.

Admittedly, there are days when I feel like the mayor of Galatia. Some days I begin to think that the gospel means I am saved by the work of Jesus *plus* the fact that I try to be a good guy. But that's not true. Being a caring husband, father, friend, or psychiatrist does not add to Jesus' work. It's the work of Jesus alone that saves me, and that justifies me—plus nothing!

Clearly, a child of God should try to reflect his Father's nature, but this doesn't mean that a gift to World Vision to feed the poor will gain acceptance by God. Loving behavior should flow from the belief that you are totally accepted, totally forgiven, and that God will never leave you no matter what trials you may face.

When people first experience a revelation of the Father's love, they are often overwhelmed with the realization that an infinite Father is deeply in love with them. But soon the distractions of work and family, a needy child, or a vulnerable friend intrude; schoolwork has to be done, the mortgage needs to be paid. Slowly, the thrilling reality of God's love and presence begins to fade away due to the cares of life. People forget the feeling of being cherished by God. They slip back into trying to fill their emptiness with money, career success, babies, or romantic relationships. It won't work, because only a Father-child relationship with God can give you what you ultimately need.

Looking at the Father's "Crazy Love"

In Victor Hugo's classic book, *Les Miserables,* Jean Valjean is sent to jail for almost twenty years for stealing a loaf of bread. During his years of slavery he slowly progresses into a bitter man, condemning everyone, including God. Jean Valjean's experience is summed up in the words, "Human society had done him nothing but injury; never had he seen anything of her but the wrathful face she calls justice, . . . showing it to those she strikes down. No man had ever touched him except to bruise him. All his contact with men had been by blows."

After Jean Valjean's release, an elderly priest allows him to eat and sleep in his home. During the middle of the night, Jean steals some silver from the priest's home and escapes through a hole in the garden wall. The next day some military police grab him because he is "acting like a fugitive." When they search him and find the silver, they are sure he is a thief, but he defends himself by saying that the priest gave it to him. The police drag him to the priest's house to verify his story. As he is dragged back to the scene of his crime, Jean Valjean is sullen and entirely dejected. He wonders, since he had received nineteen years in prison for stealing a loaf of bread, whether he is now doomed to die in a dark prison cell. But when the old priest sees him he hobbles over to him and says, "Ah, there you are! I'm glad to see you. But I gave you the candlesticks, too, which are silver like the rest and would bring you two hundred francs. Why didn't you take them along with your cutlery?"

Jean Valjean is unable to speak. And even after the police release him, he still cannot believe it. As he shrinks back, the priest goes to the mantel, takes the prized silver candlesticks down and says, "My friend . . . before you go away, here are your candlesticks. Take them." Then the priest says good-bye, telling the trembling Jean to "go in peace," and that the next time he comes to visit he should use the front door rather than the garden escape route.

As Jean Valjean leaves he is almost on the verge of fainting because he is so overwhelmed by the priest's loving gesture. He has not seen this kind of love for decades, and he had come to believe that it was not possible.

Such love *is* astounding, because it is so rare. True unconditional love is hard to come by.

That is why God's love seems so bizarre, so crazy, to many people, because they have never experienced that kind of love; it has no analogy in their experience. It is like a foreign language; it makes no sense to them.

Another reason the Father's love seems so peculiar is because our own love is shallow. If we are honest, we realize sooner or later that much of our "love" is really disguised need. Most of our kindnesses are self-serving attempts to surround ourselves with support. It is hard to imagine a Being who loves us with a love we are not capable of showing. But that is precisely the kind of Father our God is.

Avoiding God and Avoiding Shame

If you are unsure of the Father's impression of your moral state, you will not go to him with your fears and problems. You will not let him love you because you will be anticipating his rejection and disapproval.

Amy is a twenty-five-year-old stockbroker. She first came to me because of trouble with her husband, Jon, who was very withdrawn and unmotivated. She admitted that she would occasionally snap at him, and that he would react by withdrawing and leaving home for a few hours. When she realized that she had been unfair to him, she felt very guilty. In fact, she'd continue to feel guilty for a week.

And whenever she felt guilty, she stopped praying. Why? Because she had an unconscious belief that once she did something wrong, she should avoid the Father until she demonstrated to him that she could do better. She was punishing herself with a week of isolation, during which she was always more susceptible to other weaknesses.

But God does not ask us to punish ourselves in isolation in order to gain his forgiveness; he wants us to gain forgiveness in order to escape punishment. He extends his love, forgiveness, and support in the hope that we will feel secure and supported enough to eventually take some healthy and godly steps in our lives. It is very hard to give up unhealthy crutches without strong support. God wants to give his care so we can release what hinders us. Only when we are confident of God's acceptance and presence can we live lives that are pleasing to him, because "without [him we] can do nothing" (John 15:5 KJV).

Discerning the Source of Your Expectations

Another reason some people lose their sense of security with God is because they lapse back into their old father paradigms. They act as if

God's expectations are similar to the expectations of their earthly fathers, or employers, or teachers. They forget that God is an entirely different type of being.

In life, we meet father models who set goals for us. For example, one of my friends is a high school baseball coach. Occasionally we talk about the game and his coaching techniques, and I have even gone to see him in action. He is fairly tough on his young men, and he demands their full effort and concentration.

But he clearly expects a level of performance that is within each player's capabilities. He asks the pitcher to work on his curveball. He tells the right fielder to go to the batting cage more often, and tells the baserunner who is regularly picked off to pay better attention to the pitcher when he's on base. He asks his players to do things they *can* do, not what they *can't* do. In fact, most of what he asks, they can achieve with only a moderate amount of effort.

But God isn't that way. He does not merely reveal to us the next small step on the road to improvement. He doesn't say that "a little less hatred is fine," or that he'd like us to show "a bit more concern" for others. God's standards are perfection. Frankly, his standards are impossible for us fallen human beings to achieve. That does not mean we should be discouraged by our failures or surprised by our sinfulness. God isn't. He's not surprised or overwhelmed. He knows our weaknesses and loves us just the same, and if we are his children through faith in Christ, then when he looks at us he sees nothing but purity.

The demands of those around us often rob us of our sense of security. Family, friends, children, jobs, and support groups can place unreasonable demands on us, and if we do not perform the way others expect us to, we can begin to feel that all those people are right—and that we have not only disappointed them, but God.

Some Christians teach that acceptance of Christ should bring about immediate and thorough changes in a person's behavior, producing an instant "saint." The reality is that some problems take months or even years to work through. Should people who are working on difficult problems be kept outside of the Father's love until they shape up? Of course not. The fact is that none of us is ever completely "shaped up." And if we avoid God during the process of getting ourselves into shape, we will lose the power to improve ourselves.

When the Bible Can Be the Worst Book in the World

I regularly talk to people who say they are Christians, but yet who have no interest in reading the Bible.

Ellen is a thirty-four-year-old pharmaceutical saleswoman who had thought, because she'd heard that I was a man of faith, that I would be a "safe" counselor. During our initial sessions she tried to impress me with her efforts to be a "good Christian." She worked into our conversation the fact that she had been reading her Bible again.

"Did it help you or make you feel worse?" I asked.

She was stunned by the question. I'm sure she thought, *Of course it helped me. It's the Bible. It's not supposed to make you feel worse.*

But then she sat back quietly and thought about the question for a full minute. Finally, she said, "Worse." Tears filled her eyes. "Much worse," she added.

She had been reading the Scriptures in the belief that they would tell her what to do. As she read, she found that she was supposed to feed the hungry, clothe the naked, visit criminals in prison, and take care of widows and orphans. When she thought of all these expectations, she was discouraged. She never gave clothes to the poor because her old clothes went to her younger sister. She was afraid to visit criminals. And she didn't know any orphans. She occasionally helped care for her mother, a widow of five years who struggled with severe arthritis. But generally, the majority of her mother's care was given by two sisters who lived much nearer to her.

Ellen's Bible reading made her feel pretty low. Of all the things the Bible told her to do, she was only doing one of them—and even that was being done better by her sisters.

But it gets worse; she also read about the things she was not supposed to do. She read that she wasn't supposed to be bitter, to call people "fools," to lust, gossip, or forsake going to church, but she had done all those things—within the last month! Reading the Bible pointed out her misdeeds, and made each seem like a portrait of failure. Needless to say, she soon stopped reading the Scriptures.

What went wrong? Why do so many millions of people worldwide derive comfort from the Scriptures while others feel more rejected by God after reading them?

I believe the key is reading the instructions of the Bible through the eyes of the gospel—that is, in the light of the fact that the Father totally accepts you because you have accepted Jesus' work as the payment for your sins.

For example, the person who believes that God totally accepts him does not feel attacked when he reads all the things God wants him to do. He knows that the gospel anticipates his limited capacities and his time constraints. If anything, the one who reads the Bible in the light of the gospel is impressed with the depths of God's patience and forgiveness, because he sees the purity and majesty of God so clearly.

The Importance of Finding a "Safe Place"

If you have had a tragic father experience, it may be hard for you to trust others. Therefore, it is important that you deal with individuals who are trained to create safe places where emotional healing can take place.

While there are many possible "safe relationships," I want to emphasize the usefulness of a professional counselor. If you have suffered any major father trauma (beatings or constant spankings, sexual abuse, regular emotional abuse, or early father loss), it is very likely that you would benefit from professional help.

What should the "safe place" be like? First, you should feel that you can go at your own pace. It is important that you don't feel subject to your counselor's agenda, and the counselor should be willing to slow things down if you begin to feel overwhelmed. The counseling environment should be private, and the material you discuss regarded as entirely confidential. It should be a place where you can be ruthlessly honest, share your mistakes, and still feel like you have value. Certainly, counselors should be allowed to respectfully share their concerns about your lifestyle if they see unhealthy behaviors, but you should always experience an "umbrella of acceptance."[1]

One of the benefits of experiencing a safe place is that it helps you trust and love the Father more. Why does this happen? Because it is easier to believe that the eternal Father loves you unconditionally when you see that a father-like counselor is willing to accept you—even when he (or she) knows your darkest failures. It is easier to believe that acceptance exists in an unseen realm when you see it in the visible world.

Occasionally, people of faith struggle with who they should see for counseling: a pastor, priest, psychologist, social worker, or psychiatrist. Some conservative churches feel that it is important to go to the pastor over any other type of professional counselor. However, the Father gives gifts to everyone, and I believe it is often helpful to have input from both pastoral and nonpastoral counselors. They are typically trained to see different types of problems. Why should we believe that God intends to give support from only one source? Help does not have to be an either/or proposition.

Whoever you see should have some training in psychology. In our earlier sections, we discussed the psychological implications of father deprivation. Typically, subtle effects of paternal deprivation will be best seen by those who are trained to recognize them. While psychology does overlap with theology, it is not simply a secular replacement. Psychology shows other aspects of emotional problems because it has different problem filters. Both psychology and theology can help bring insight and comfort.

If you are going to a counselor to deal with your father issues it may be more helpful to see a male therapist. It may help to soften unpleasant male memories by having a healthy male relationship. Of course, if you are uncomfortable with men, see a female therapist. While the goal is to eventually heal any male-avoidance tendencies, a key first priority is to "connect" with your therapist. Since a therapist plays a mentor role, and is, therefore, "father-like," you may begin to place your father feelings onto a female therapist by virtue of her mentoring authority.

If you have experienced serious abuse you will need more than an occasional counseling session. As a victim of abuse, you will have the opportunity to learn a great deal about yourself as you process your pain through therapy, but you will not be able to achieve such insight with brief therapy. Therefore, try to find a professional who will be available for the long term. Therapists who plan to retire or relocate or who spend entire summers vacationing may not be the best for you. In the course of intense therapy, you will develop a close relationship with your therapist, and long interruptions in therapy can make you feel like you've lost a loved one, which only complicates your struggles.

If you decide to pursue counseling, you will need to think about money. Many insurance plans have poor mental health coverage. Many allow a set number of visits or force you to see the least expensive counselors. Fees for a pastoral counselor, social worker, or master's level psychologist are often least expensive and are sometimes paid by a church. Psychologists with Ph.D.'s are more costly, and psychiatrists, since they have at least eight years of medical and psychology training, are the most expensive. If the cost per month exceeds 10 percent of your income, it is probably too high for your budget.

Finally, don't be afraid to shop around. If you don't feel a connection with one therapist, perhaps you should try another one. Over time, however, you should settle into a therapeutic relationship with someone. Unstable counseling relationships will not help you work through your father issues or help you establish stable personal relationships!

19

A Final Word

. . . .

*M*any years ago I was praying alone during my Friday lunch hour. It was the day after the midnight conversation in which my father had shared his own struggles. As I said before, I appreciated his intimacy and honesty, but the realization of my father's vulnerability was very unsettling.

That day, I began the process of weaning myself from my father to lean more on God and give more of my concerns over to his fatherhood.

As I got up to leave from my time of prayer I had a strong sense that I should open my Bible. I opened randomly to the first chapter of the Gospel of Mark.

When I saw the page I had opened to, I started to turn it, thinking that all I would read in the first chapter of Mark was a long genealogy. But as I reached for the edge of the page, I had the sense that I should stay right where I was.

I looked down, and immediately saw the words of Mark 1:11. They seemed to jump off the page: "And a voice came from heaven, 'You are my Son, whom I love; with you I am well pleased.'" I had read these words before, but now they were words *to me*. Surely they were originally spoken to Jesus, but they became intensely personal to me in that moment. I sank to the floor with a realization of the intense majesty of God and the meaning of those words for me. The God of creation, the God of the seas and the heavens, regarded me as his child!

Someone who believes this consistently will not live the same old way. He will think in new ways, because his orphan feelings will melt. He will do things he never thought possible and in ways that were previously beyond his capability. In the affection and fatherhood of God, life fears, even fear of death, can lift, leaving you to embrace a life that is truly worth living. Filled with the love of God, you will finally have the support to release the pain of childhood. Adults who never had the chance to laugh as children can experience childlike joy.

If you never had a safe, joyous childhood place, find it now. Be a kid for a while. Put away all your seriousness, or your compulsive need to be perfect, to please others, to know everything, or to work yourself to exhaustion.

When was the last time you had a water-gun fight? When was the last time you laughed so loud that people turned around and looked at you?

Childlike lightness and adventure remind me of our instruction to come to God as a little child—a child who lives without fear, who lives clothed in joy.

For Meditation and Personal Insight

. . . .

Your Life

1. Write your life story. Pay particular attention to your earliest memories, especially those involving your father.
2. What feelings were you experiencing during the events in your story? Review what you wrote and make sure you were in touch with more than just raw information.
3. As a child and adolescent, what conclusions did you draw about yourself, your father, your parents' marriage, the world, and the future?
4. Would you say that you feel like an emotional orphan? What experiences have made you feel this way? Have you ever been able to talk about these experiences with anyone?
5. In your life has your father been a comforter? List the major trials of your life. During how many of those times was your father there for you?
6. Some orphans live every day by ignoring their feelings and sacrificing themselves. Is this you? Do you care for yourself and your needs, or just for everyone else?
7. How are you functioning in your major relationships? Are you intimate with people? Do you fear your boss or your teachers more than others do?
8. Examine your sexuality. Do you feel the need to apologize for being a woman? Do you use your sexuality to try to heal emotional wounds? Is your father involved in these wounds or insecurities?

Your Father's Life

1. Write your father's life story. Describe in as much detail as possible his relationship with his father.
2. What was your father's household like when he was growing up?
3. What were the major events of your father's life? What were his joys and discouragements?
4. Who are your father's friends? Are they close friendships?
5. Who were your father's most significant mentors? Were they manipulative? Kind? Wise? Unwise?
6. How did your father discipline you?
7. Describe your father's work responsibility. Did he like work or did he hate it?
8. Were you a planned child? Did your father ever comment on this?
9. What are your father's major strengths? His weaknesses?
10. Would you say your father is more or less emotionally healthy than his father? On what do you base your answer?
11. Did your father make you dislike your body or your gender? What did he do or say to make you feel this way? What impact, if any, did his comments have on you?
12. Does your father encourage or discourage you with his comments? Have you ever discussed the quality of your relationship with your father?
13. Describe the relationship between your mother and father. How do you communicate with each of them?
14. Does your father ever kiss or hug you? Does he shake your hand?

God the Father

1. Jesus is the spokesman for the Father (John 14:10); he speaks the Father's words. Where Scripture gives Jesus' words, remember that they are also the Father's words.
2. Imagine God the Father speaking the words of Jesus directly to you right now. What would that mean to you?

3. Forget your creed or childhood doctrine about God for a moment and look inside. Do you experience God as a force and impersonal power, or as a very real personality?
4. Do you resent the Father for the things you have suffered, the lonely, vulnerable experiences you have had to endure?
5. If you could ask God three questions, what would they be?
6. Do you believe God can be trusted to care for you?
7. What is your fantasy of heaven? What will happen the first five minutes you are there?

Endnotes

....

Chapter One: Everybody Needs a Father

1. Robert Bly, "The Hunger for the King in a Time with No Father," *Fathers: Sons and Daughters,* Charles S. Scull, ed. (Los Angeles: Jeremy P. Tarcher, 1992), 60.

2. William F. Hodges, *Interventions for Children of Divorce* (New York: Wiley, 1991), 1.

3. A. E. Hotchner, *Sophia, Living and Loving* (New York: William Morrow and Company, 1979), 29–32, 241.

4. Hotchner, 95.

5. Hotchner, 242.

6. Hotchner, 241; Christopher Andersen, *Father, the Figure and the Force* (New York: Warner, 1983), 28–29.

7. Hotchner, 15.

8. Hotchner, 11.

9. Ruth Ann Seilhamer and T. Jacob, "Family Factors and Adjustments of Children of Alcoholics," in *Children of Alcoholics*, Michael Windle and John S. Searles, eds. (New York: Guilford Press, 1990), 176–77.

10. Brandt F. Steele, "Abusive Fathers," in *Father and Child*, Stanley Cath, A. Gurwitt, J. M. Ross, eds. (Boston: Wiley, 1982), 481.

11. *The International Cyclopedia of Music and Musicians,* Robert Sabin, ed., 9th ed. (New York: Dodd, Mead & Co., 1964), 1049.

12. Sabin, 1049.

13. Stuart Feder, *My Father's Song* (New Haven: Yale, 1992), 285–87, 379.

14. Victoria Secunda, *Women and Their Fathers* (New York: Delacorte, 1992), xii–xiv.

Chapter Three: The Search for Lost Fathering

1. Steve Alessandri, Ph.D., Prof. of Pediatrics and Psychiatry, Medical College of Pennsylvania. Personal communication, June 24, 1993.

2. D. Burlingham, "The Preoedipal Infant-Father Relationship," in *Psychoanalytic Study of the Child,* vol. 28 (New Haven: Yale University Press, 1973), 36.

3. Leonard Shengold, *Soul Murder: The Effects of Childhood Abuse and Deprivation* (New York: Ballantine Books, 1989). These summary statements pervade the entire text.

Chapter Five: The Father's Role in His Children's Sexual Identity

1. Margo Maine, *Father Hunger: Fathers, Daughters and Food* (Carlsbad, Calif.: Gurze, 1991), xi–xv.

2. Ibid.

3. Ibid.

4. Maine, xii–xiv.

5. Nancy Chodorow, *Feminism and Psychoanalytic Theory* (New Haven: Yale, 1989), 50–51.

6. Christopher P. Andersen, *Father, the Figure and the Force* (New York: Warner, 1983), 88–89.

7. Ibid.

8. L. B. Apperson and W. G. McAdoo, "Parental Factors in the Childhood of Homosexuals," *Journal of Abnormal Psychology* 73 (1968), 201–6; E. Bene, "On the Genesis of Male Homosexuality: An Attempt at Clarifying the Role of the Parents," *British Journal of Psychiatry* 111 (1965), 803–13; D. G. Brown, "Homosexuality and Family Dynamics," *Bulletin of the Menninger Clinic* 27 (1963): 227–32; R. B. Evans, "Childhood Parental Relationships of Homosexual Men," *Journal of Consulting and Clinical Psychology* 33 (1969), 129–35; I. Bieber et. al., *Homosexuality: A Psychoanalytic Study* (New York: Basic Books, 1962).

Chapter Seven: Shining the Light on Orphan Psychology

1. While the material in this chapter is my own, I want to thank Dr. Ed Welch of the Christian Counseling and Education Foundation and Pastor Jack Miller, both of Philadelphia, for promoting the theme of the orphan. They made me see the value of meditating on the idea.

2. John Weil, *Early Deprivation of Empathic Care* (Madison, Conn.: International Universities Press, 1992), 1–2; Robert Zingg, "Feral Man and Extreme Cases of Isolation," *The American Journal of Psychology* LIII, no. 4 (October 1940): 487–517; J. Langmeier and Z. Matejcek, *Psychological Deprivation in Childhood* (St. Lucia: Queenland Press, 1975) 3rd ed. (English), 35–45.

3. One wonders how far one can go in applying these stories to higher functioning people, and the subtle "orphan-like" emotions healthy people experience. Some of the reactions of these children could be due to neurological changes and greater familiarity with animal "culture." Nevertheless, I think such stories are powerful tools for reflection, and that is their purpose here.

4. Robert Zingg and A. Gesell, *Wolf Children and Human Child* (New York, London: Harper and Brothers, 1940).

5. Langmeier and Matejcek, 37–38.

6. Langmeier and Matejcek, 68.

7. Zingg, 513, 38.

8. Zingg, 500–5, 507–17; Langmeier and Matejcek, 37–38.

9. Jean-Marc-Gaspard Itard, *The Wild Boy of Aveyron*, trans. George and Muriel Humphrey (New York: Appleton-Century-Crofts, 1962), 3–4.

10. Itard, 9–10.

11. Itard, 88.

12. Itard, 8, 88–89.

13. Langmeier and Matejcek, 44–45.

14. Weil, 110–13.

Chapter Eight: The Orphan's Need for Security

1. Charles Dickens, *Oliver Twist*, 1867 ed. (New York: Bantam Books, 1990), 1–2.

2. Peter Ackroyd, *Dickens* (New York: Harper Collins, 1990), 838.

3. Charles Dickens, *Oliver Twist* (inside flap front page).

4. P. Tacon, *My Child Now: An Action Plan on Behalf of Children without Families* (New York: United Nations International Children's Educational Fund, 1981); P. Tacon, *Regional Program for Latin America and the Caribbean* (New York: United Nations International Children's Educational Fund, 1983); as quoted in Lewis Aptekar, "The Psychology of Columbian Street Children," *International Journal of Health Services* 19, no. 2 (1989): 295.

5. L. M. Cortes, "Temas Colombianas: La Metamorfosis del 'Chino de la Called," *Editextos* (Bogota, 1969); A. Pardo and E. Vergara, "Estudio Medico–Social de la Vagrancia Infantil de Bogota," *Revista Colombiana de Psychiatria* 1, no. 1 (1964): 37–67.

6. J. Kirk Felsman, "Abandoned Children: A Reconsideration," *Children Today* (May–June 1984): 16.

7. Aptekar, 305–6.

8. Mark Connolly, "Adrift in the City: A Comparative Study of Street Children in Bogota, Colombia, and Guatemala City," *Homeless Children: The Watchers and the Waiters* (Haworth Press, 1990).

9. Aptekar, 298–99.

Chapter Ten: Why Can't I Love God Like I Want To?

1. Ana-Maria Rizzuto, *The Birth of the Living God* (Chicago: University of Chicago, 1979), 4.

2. Paul Vitz, "The Psychology of Atheism and Christian Spirituality," *Anthropotes* 6 (1990): 99.

3. Ibid.

4. Antony Flew, *A Dictionary of Philosophy* (New York: St. Martin's Press, 1979), 133–34.

5. Colin Brown, *Philosophy and the Christian Faith* (London: Tyndale, 1968), 138–39.

6. Brown, 225–26.

7. Brown, 183.

8. Richard P. McBrien, *Catholicism* (Minneapolis: Winston, 1981), 115, 255, 330.

9. J. W. Murray, *My Life without God* (Nashville: Thomas Nelson, 1982), 8 (as quoted in Vitz, 100).

Chapter Eleven: Bible Fathers from Adam to Jacob

1. Bruce Waltke, notes from the course titled "Understanding the Old Testament," Lecture 1, produced in 1979 by the Institute of Theological Studies, P.O. Box 1000, Grand Rapids, MI, 49501.

2. Derek Kidner, *Genesis,* Tyndale Old Testament Commentaries, D. J. Wiseman, gen. ed., vol. I (London: Tyndale, 1967), 60.

3. Gordon J. Wenham, "The Coherence of the Flood Narrative," *Vetus Testamentum* 28 (1978):336–48 as quoted in Isaac M. Kikawada and Arthur Quinn's *Before Abraham Was* (Nashville: Abingdon, 1985), 104.

Chapter Twelve: Bible Fathers from Joseph to Moses

1. Leon J. Wood, *A Survey of Israel's History,* rev. by David O'Brien (Grand Rapids: Zondervan, 1986), 93.

2. Baruch Margalit, "Why King Mesha of Moab Sacrificed His Oldest Son," *Biblical Archaeology Review* 12 (November/December 1986): 62–63.

Chapter Thirteen: David—The Adopted Son of God

1. Paul Tournier, *Creative Suffering,* trans. Edwin Hudson (San Francisco: Harper and Row, 1982), 2. See also Pierre Rentchnick, "Orphans Lead the World," *Medecines et hygiene* (November 26, 1975).

2. Gerald R. Ford, *A Time to Heal* (New York: Harper and Row, 1978). (As quoted in Andersen, 9–10).

3. Tournier, 2.

4. Tournier, 4.

5. Haynal et. al. (see table at end of book), 121–24.

6. Tournier, 12–13.

Chapter Fourteen: The Day the Father Came to Earth

1. Isaiah 9:6. The alternative translation is from George B. Gray, *A Critical and Exegetical Commentary on the Book of Isaiah* I-XXXXIX (Edinburgh: T & T Clark, 1912), 174.

2. Kenneth Bailey, *A Study of Some Lucan Parables in the Light of Oriental Life and Poetic Style,* Doctoral Thesis presented to the Faculty of Concordia Seminary (St. Louis: 1972), 2. Hereafter D. T.; Kenneth Bailey, *The Cross and the Prodigal* (St. Louis: Concordia, 1973), 10.

3. Bailey, D. T., 7; Bailey, *The Cross,* 31–33.

4. Bailey, *The Cross,* 42, 43, 54.

5. Bailey, *The Cross,* 69.

6. Joachim Jeremias, *The Lord's Prayer,* trans. John Reumann (Philadelphia: Fortress, 1964), 19.

7. *60 Minutes,* "Medical Miracle," July 18, 1993. 524 West 57th Street, New York, NY 10019, 16–22.

8. *60 Minutes,* 17.

9. *60 Minutes,* 18.

10. *60 Minutes,* 19.

Chapter Fifteen: Putting Your Heart Back Together

1. Roger E. Axtell, *Gestures: The Do's and Taboos of Body Language Around the World* (New York: John Wiley, 1991), 42–43.

2. Axtell, 46.

3. Robert L. Griswold, *Fatherhood in America* (New York: Basic Books, 1993), 11.

4. Griswold, 10.

5. Griswold, 28.

6. Griswold, 57.

7. Griswold, 43.

8. Marilee Pierce Dunker, *Man of Vision, Woman of Prayer* (Nashville: Thomas Nelson, 1980), 184, 194.

Chapter Sixteen: Dealing with Anger and Healing the Pain

1. Frances E. Schoeninger and Douglas W. Schoeninger, "Working Through to Forgiveness," *The Journal of Christian Healing* 15, no. 2 & 3 (Summer/Fall 1993): 52.

2. Mary S. Cernay, "Imagery and Grief Work," *Bulletin of the Menninger Clinic* (1985): 36–37.

Chapter Seventeen: Maximizing Your Father Relationship

1. Bill Hybels and Bobb Biehl, "Mentoring," Focus on the Family Tapes, CS680 (1992).

2. Sharan Merriam, "Mentors and Proteges: A Critical Review of the Literature," *Adult Education Quarterly* 33, no. 3 (1983): 162.

3. Ibid.

4. Richard P. Kluft, "Treating the Patient Who Has Been Sexually Exploited by a Previous Therapist," *Psychiatric Clinics of North America* 12, no. 2 (June 1989): 486.

5. Charles Stanley, "The Burden of Emotional Baggage," Second International Congress of Christian Counseling. Atlanta, November 13, 1992. Copies available from Fuller Theoloical Seminary, Media Services, Box 234, Pasadena, CA 91182.

Chapter Eighteen: The Everlasting Father

1. Ralph Eckardt, personal communication, Drexel Hill, Pennsylvania, August 18, 1992.